WITH EVERYTHING WE'VE GOT

A PERSONAL ANTHOLOGY OF YIDDISH POETRY

WITH EVERYTHING WE'VE GOT

A PERSONAL ANTHOLOGY OF YIDDISH POETRY

EDITED AND TRANSLATED BY
RICHARD J. FEIN

INTRODUCTION AND BIOGRAPHICAL SKETCHES BY
SETH L. WOLITZ

TECHNICAL PREPARATION OF THE YIDDISH TEXT BY
HARRY BOCHNER & DAVID BRAUN

HOST PUBLICATIONS
AUSTIN, TX

Host Publications, Inc. copyright © 2009

English translation copyright © 2009 by Richard J. Fein

All poems by Moyshe-Leyb Halpern by permission of Isaac Halpern.

"She with the Cold, Marble Breasts," by Anna Margolin, with permission of Abraham Novershtern.

All poems by H. Leivick by permission of Ida Leivick.

All poems by Abraham Sutzkever by permission of the author (through the good offices of Ruth Wisse).

"Dream Canaan," by Abo Stolzenberg, by permission of Gabriel Stolzenberg.

Despite efforts to trace copyright holders, in a few cases this has proven impossible. The publisher would be interested in hearing from any copyright holders not herein acknowledged.

Host Publications, Inc. 277 Broadway, Suite 210, New York, NY 10007

Layout and Design:	Joe Bratcher & Anand Ramaswamy
Cover Art:	Wojciech Ćwiertniewicz
Cover Design:	Anand Ramaswamy
Inside Book Sketches:	Yosl Cutler

First Edition

Library of Congress Cataloging-in-Publication Data

With everything we've got : a personal anthology of Yiddish poetry / edited and translated by Richard J. Fein ; introduction and biographical sketches by Seth Wolitz ; technical preparation of the Yiddish text by Harry Bochner & David Braun. -- 1st ed.
    p. cm.
Includes bibliographical references.
Summary: "[A bilingual English/Yiddish poetry anthology]"--Provided by publisher.
ISBN-13: 978-0-924047-45-9 (hardcover : alk. paper)
ISBN-10: 0-924047-45-3 (hardcover : alk. paper)
ISBN-13: 978-0-924047-64-0 (pbk. : alk. paper)
ISBN-10: 0-924047-64-X (pbk. : alk. paper)
1. Yiddish poetry. 2. Yiddish poetry--Translations into English. I. Fein, Richard J., 1929- II. Wolitz, Seth L.

PJ5191.E3W58 2008
839'.11308--dc22
                                        2008035864

BOOKS BY RICHARD J. FEIN

POETRY

Selected Poems of Yankev Glatshteyn (translations)

Kafka's Ear

At the Turkish Bath

To Move into the House

Ice like Morsels

I Think of Our Lives: New and Selected Poems

Mother Tongue

Reversion

PROSE

Robert Lowell

The Dance of Leah

"*Listen'd to keep, to sing, now translating the notes,*
Following you my brother."

– Walt Whitman, *Out of the Cradle Endlessly Rocking*

TABLE OF CONTENTS

* Indented poems by Richard J. Fein

תוכן

ACKNOWLEDGMENTS

Poems in this anthology have previously appeared in the journals *Afn shvel*, *The Dirty Goat*, *Jewish Currents*, *Kerem*, *Midstream*, *Present Tense*, *Seneca Review*, *Shirim*, *Tsukunft*, and in my books: *Kafka's Ear*, *At the Turkish Bath*, *To Move into the House*, *Ice like Morsels*, *I Think of Our Lives*, *Mother Tongue*, *Reversion*.

I wish to express my appreciation of Larry Rosenwald and Seth Wolitz, each a conscience of translation, and both old enough to remember the motto of the animal explorer Frank Buck – *Bring 'Em Back Alive*.

I also want to thank George Kalogeris, Marcia Karp and Steven Sher for helping me shape this book.

With thanks to Solon Beinfeld, Harry Bochner and David Braun for their knowledge of Yiddish and their alertness to the ways Yiddish poets play with the language.

And thanks to Joe Bratcher and Anand Ramaswamy for their editorial skills and sensitivities.

NOTE

The poets are presented chronologically, except for the last one, Abo Stolzenberg. The poems of each poet are in an order that seems fit to me.

I have not included here any of the translations that are in my *Selected Poems of Yankev Glatshteyn*.

For Rabbi Ben-Zion Gold

PREFACE

This book is a gathering of Yiddish poems that have entered my life and work. This collection came out of my need to read Yiddish poetry and then – through that engagement we call translation – to give voice to what this poetry has meant to me.

By "a personal anthology of Yiddish poetry" I mean that this collection is not representative of Yiddish poetry, perhaps not even of the work of the poets included here. But it is a collection of Yiddish poems I have been driven to translate over the last three decades, ever since I learned Yiddish and returned to writing poetry. I have not distinguished here between close translations and freer translations. The collection also contains several of my own poems which led to or came out of those translations, or bear upon my attachment to Yiddish and Yiddish poetry. Often in my own books of poems a translation and a poem of mine are face to face because they speak to one another. Similar conversations go on in this book. And then there is the internal dialogue, you might say, between a translation and its Yiddish original.

This book is not a homage to Yiddish poetry, but a book born out of my intercourse with Yiddish and Yiddish poetry. Translation is lust – a way of possessing the Yiddish poem – of being more intimate with its letters and words, and then discovering in the process the seeding of one's own English. The book (I hope) shows the ongoing powers of Yiddish poetry, how that poetry can be read for itself and how that poetry has helped an American poet to write his own poems. Deep into my own work, I found myself having a new take on a remark by T.S. Eliot in his essay "Tradition and the Individual Talent" (though he didn't have Yiddish poetry in mind when he made it):

> *We shall often find that not only the best, but the most individual parts of [a poet's] work may be those in which the dead poets, his ancestors, assert their immortality most vigorously.*

Might not that remark come into play even for someone writing out of his relationship to Yiddish poetry? This book can also be read as a sequence, one voice in contact with different voices of Yiddish poetry, or as a collection of Yiddish poetry with responsa, as a friend of mine puts it.

I have a dual feeling about these translations. They are renderings from another language, and at the same time they also seem to be my own poems (absorptions that have become part of me). Indeed, my own poems sometimes seem to be alternative forms of Yiddish poems. I think of the way two trees coming out of one base, rising to their respective heights, where their branches and foliage mingle, seem to be two trees and one tree at the same time. I have at times entertained the illusion that I am a Yiddish poet who, as it happens, writes in English.

The deepest thing I can say about Yiddish is that it is something that happened to me. For me, Yiddish words are as much about the space they occupy in place of English as about what they say.

Making Vocabulary Lists While Learning Yiddish

The letters bundle
down the page –
curling, squarish, stooped, arched,
no capitals,
crooked, paunched, bowed, hooked, rigid,
right-angled, festooned, knotted, flourishing.

I cannot glide over them;
they flag the eye.

וו   (*v*ovn)

I wade in these words
slithering in and out of meaning,

אָ   (aleph-*o*)

ciphers teasing
or garnering sense,

ר   (*r*eysh)

while with English
the prim letters stay in place,
sewn into the word.

Stirred into Yiddish,
steeped in its juices

ט   (*t*es)

I soak up its sounds,
and savor the *word!* –

וואָרט   (*vort*)

AN EXILIC HOMELAND: YIDDISH POETRY

The Jewish grand narrative begins in exile, whether: (1) cosmic – the kabbalistic model of Rabbi Isaac Luria (1534-1572), where the universe was rent in a catastrophe separating man from God; or (2) Biblical – the expulsion of Adam and Eve from the Garden of Eden; or (3) the terrestrial and historical exiles of Jews from their homeland, and their endless wanderings. Liberations are rare – and costly – but the great escape from the Egyptian exile and slavery constitutes the beginning of the Jewish people and their unique embrace of the Ten Commandments and the one God. Text becomes the real Jewish homeland and Israel is its ark. Jewry has lived from exile to exile, subjugation to subjugation, with momentary liberations. The Jewish prose epic, the Bible, essentially relates how a defeated folk became an ethical nation – even a power – and then fell again into exile. This narrative differs from most other nations that pride themselves as victors, descendants of gods (or at least their royal houses), with leaders who are brave warriors and conquerors. The latter grand narrative of divine descent and assuredness, the Hellenic model, found its first poetic voice in the Greek epic of the *Iliad*, and appears later in Roman culture in Virgil's *Aeneid*, and in ancient India in the magnificent Sanskrit epic, *Mahabharata*. Jewish culture cleaves then to a different worldview and tradition from the grand poetic narratives of most other nations, and this culture includes its own aesthetics and poetry.

Jewish poetry in Hebrew fills sections of the Bible and continues to influence the ethics of later Jewish poetry, repeatedly providing themes, imagery, prosody and the grand narrative. Jewish poetry was never closed to contiguous influences, and in Spain the Jews adopted Arabic meters and forms, producing the refined medieval Hebrew poetry that lasted until 1492 and the exile of the Jews.

For almost five hundred years, Ashkenazic Jewry – the Jews of central and Eastern Europe and now the majority of Jews in the New World, in comparison with Sephardic Jewry, descendants of the Spanish exile produced few works of aesthetic interest, considering secular poetry a negative force, a frivolity. The Eastern European Jews spoke Yiddish, the evolved German language brought from the Rhineland where Jews lived as exiles since late Roman times and from which they fled during the Crusades to more hospitable settings in Poland. There, given both limited political and cultural autonomy, they developed their unique religious lifestyle. Surrounded by Slavic, the German tongue evolved into Yiddish to accommodate the distinct features of Jewish life. Yiddish was a language of daily life, written down mainly for men and women illiterate in Hebrew. It expressed the needs and wants of a population but not its intellectual or theological concerns.

Only with the arrival of the Enlightenment in Eastern Europe did the Jews in the mid-nineteenth century return to aesthetic interests and initiate the revival of poetry and secular literature. The *maskilim*, Jewish adherents of Western Enlightenment principles, recognized the power and freedom of aesthetic space to explore and newly interpret the human condition. The *maskilim*, the first poets of the revival, used Hebrew mainly for their lyrical impulses, and exploited the folkic qualities of Yiddish for satirical ends, usually to mock superstition and Khasidic mystical traditions. Hebrew poetry reemerged with the advantage of a long inheritance but with a frozen tongue like Latin, whereas Yiddish was the spoken language of the majority of Ashkenazic Jewry in the nineteenth century. Traditional scholars wrote in Hebrew, but Yiddish remained the language of the people, devoid of any higher cultural function.

The new Yiddish poetry had no inherited themes, forms or imagery but the folk memory of Biblical and Rabbinic narrative texts in Hebrew and Aramaic. There were folk songs in Yiddish, lullabies, children's songs, laments of forced conscripts, songs of robbers, and religious mystical songs of the khasidim, etc., but the first conscious efforts were didactic performances using fables and satiric verse. The folk song tradition became a stable part of the new literary culture and many poets embraced the genre to express their communal sentiments, actualities and admonishments, lamentations and appreciations, creating intimacy, immediacy and assured Jewish identity, particularly in performance. The folk song poets played an important role in this highly oral culture, from Berl Broder (1817-1868), Elyokem Tsunzer (1836-1913) [*Vi lang vestu Yidl arumgeyn un handlen;* "How long will you, little Jew, go about and haggle?"], and Mark Varshavski (1848-1907) in the nineteenth century, to the last folk poet, Mordkhe Gebirtig (1877-1942), in the Cracow ghetto, [*S'brent, oy unzer orim shtetl, nebekh, brent;* "It's burning, woe! Our poor little town is burning up."]

The first conscious poets in Yiddish borrowed Western prosody, genres, rhymes, meters and themes from the surrounding cultures, mainly German and later Russian and Polish. The syllabotonic (accentual-syllabic) meter became the norm for Yiddish verse and iambic tetrameter (four feet) was the favored rhythmic verse line. The rhymes were rarely more than one syllable and only the accented same vowel and final consonant rhymed (*zog/tog*), or vowel and two consonants (*aropgerISN/ayngebISN*). Richer rhymes of one syllable, such as same consonant, vowel and consonant, or a two syllable rhyme were extremely rare. Moyshe Broderzon (1890-1956) was the master of Yiddish rhyme and his virtuosity delights for its sheer bravura, even as melancholy lurks below. Elyokem Tsunzer is thought to have introduced blank verse and this was used considerably. Assonance appears more regularly too as slant rhyme in modernist verse. Poets adopted the typical folk poetry rhyme scheme *abcb* per stanza, but the western *abab* was common too. In declamatory verse, *aabb*, or flat rhymes were favored and Avrom Goldfadn (1840-1908) in his verse plays drew full rhetorical effect from his end-stopping flat rhymes. Perets Markish introduced from Russian the poenonic foot of three short syllables and one long one, and Uri Zvi Greenberg extended the verse line for more varied rhythms, a technique many poets imitated. Moyshe Kulbak and Perets Markish imported many slavicisms to provide a more "folkic" tonality. Uri Zvi Greenberg and more religious poets heightened the Hebrew lexical presence, seeking a higher tonality. Dovid Hofshteyn and the earlier "Sweatshop Poets" favored *daytchmerisms* or imported Germanic vocabulary to add precisions and prestige. The Yiddish women poets tended to limit Hebraic lexical elements in their verses and preferred to use simpler syntactical structures. Yiddish writers – and the language itself – never felt wary of importing from the surrounding cultures what was needed to enrich the language and art of the poets for the new secular culture. The prosody, themes, imagery and styles reflect consciously the interface not only within this fermenting Yiddish culture but between itself and the surrounding cultures. The full one-hundred years of Yiddish poetry express the dreams, tensions, attractions and conflicts of Ashkenazic Jewry in its own soul, as well as its encounters with the world.

Yiddish poetry emerged like mushrooms after a rain, unexpectedly and extensively, at the end of the nineteenth century. Yitskhok Leyb Perets (1852-1915) receives the accolade in the history of Yiddish poetry as the first truly accomplished poet. He played with folkloric elements, legends, the concerns of his day, philosophical expressions of the good life, humorous verse, and the first verse novel in Yiddish, *Monish*. Well read in European literatures, by the turn of the century he was considered the central figure in Yiddish poetry, prose and verse drama. He introduced Western genres, and used poetry as the expression of the new secular Jewish life unfurling, and his range and loyalties, if at times contradictory, depict the energy of modern Yiddish culture and poetry. He embraced socialism, mysticism, realism, symbolism and neo-romanticism, the key movements in Yiddish culture. His home in Warsaw, Poland, was the national literary salon where new writers appeared, new works were declaimed, and reputations were made. Perets symbolized the revitalized diasporic Jewish culture, its validation and continuity. The new poets did not obey most of Perets' advice on verse, but in his efforts they found themes and models to develop or reject in the explosive force of this new culture. Perets sought to create a Jewish culture accommodated to Western Civilization but maintaining a balance between the old Jewish inheritance and Western modernity.

The Jews fleeing Tsarist oppression – which grew worse after the Assassination of Alexander II in 1881 – brought with them to America utopian socialist ideals, universalism, anarchism, Jewish variants of social justice and Jewish national aspirations. They felt as if they had fled Egypt, but New York and the sweatshops of the Lower East Side were less a Promised Land than even the Sinai Desert. Here modern mass existence, man reduced to serve a machine, launched Yiddish verse into the modern age with its protest poetry. The poets who expressed the collective anger and pain of physical, mental and emotional exile, particularly in the exploitative garment industry, were themselves workers, and their verses embraced the ideals of socialist universalism, demands for social justice, and the legitimacy of their cultural particularity. The strongest voice was Morris Rosenfeld (1862-1923), who used the language of everyday Yiddish speech to express the yearning needs and aspirations of his fellow workers. Yiddish poetry was concerned with issues of class consciousness, revolutionary incentives, social values and secular culture, rather than just the growth of Jewish national rights. Though there is a strong sentimental streak in this poetry, it nonetheless reveals the desperation of the working conditions: in the first person, Rosenfeld revels in seeing his child but rarely has the chance – working hours reached almost sixteen hours a day. These poems were recited at the worktables and at social meetings. They were sung and repeated continuously. This poetry is urban, collective in consciousness, secular, and proudly expressive of the working class, signaling a new Jewish identity allied to socialist universalism. Yiddish poetry in America would generally be created by Jews who came from the working classes, and who received in the Old Country a traditional Jewish religious education and encountered socialism in the cities on their way to America. The early poets in New York received the title of Sweatshop Poets, and the most popular poets associated with this school included Dovid Edelstadt (1866-1892), Joseph Boshever (1873-1915), and Morris Vinchevsky (1856-1923). Their verse excited the Jewish masses, both in America and in Europe, to the possibilities of poetry as a source of inspiration, protest, and change, a secular aesthetic alternative to traditional Judaism. To this day in Jewish Old People's Homes, the words of these poets are remembered and recited with fervor while greater Yiddish poems are forgotten.

Alongside the strong voices of social collective expression came a new group of poets in New York who took a more personal perspective in their verse. The beloved Avrom Reyzn (1876-1953) wrote moving, melancholic verse that gave legitimacy to private emotions and was rich in nostalgia for the Old Country. He mused on such themes as childhood, the sweetness and sourness of love – a new theme for Jews – failed hopes, resignation, and the sufferings of the poor. His poems were often set to music and sung as folksongs. During his long life, Reyzn was involved in all facets of Yiddish cultural production, and he was esteemed by every poetic movement that developed, both for his personality and the deftness of his lyric touch. Yehoash (1870-1927) opened Yiddish poetry to personal experience and foreign cultures. He traveled the world and transferred his experiences into Yiddish in finely wrought verse. His major contribution was the translation into Yiddish of the Bible, revealing that Yiddish could be an instrument for artistic expression.

In the years prior to World War One, Yiddish poetry fought to legitimize itself as a mature instrument of nuanced expression and delicacy, especially against the successes of Hebrew verse. The vitality of new Jewish culture in Hebrew was best evidenced in the verse of Khayim Nakhman

Bialik, the national poet, whose most popular works include a number of Biblical poems, and "In the City of Slaughter" (1906), an extraordinary dirge on a pogrom scene. Also part of this movement was the gifted Saul Tchernichovsky (1874-1943), whose nature poetry and esteem of Hellenism raised eyebrows.

Yiddish poets before World War One, especially in New York, moved to a contemporary representation of their personal concerns and urban lives. Under the influence of Russian impressionism and symbolism, German neo-Romanticism, and French Parnassians, they sought to convey the nuances of their worldview, their encounters with their emotions, and their social milieu. They were determined to create perfectly shaped poems that evinced a rich, complex yet unified mood, poems that encompassed a totality of a world. They wanted art for art's sake: to craft a work of art that was as hard and perfect as a gemstone. By 1907 the new immigrant poets in New York banded together and took on the name *Di Yunge* (The Young Ones), rejecting the Sweatshop Poets role as *vox populi*. Mani Leyb (1883-1953) captures well this new apolitical aesthetic in his wonderful sonnets – perhaps the first in Yiddish. His poetic voice is one of hushed tones, of domestic scenes under siege, of quiet desperation and the sense of exile. He brought sophistication and musicality to his poetry, and introduced new forms, particularly ballads and folklore. His poetry for children was also beloved. In contrast to Mani Leyb's quiet tones, Moshe Leyb Halpern (1886-1933) clangs with fire and impishness, providing a bold new voice like no other. He sets out to complain and mock at the same time, mixing pathos with nonsense and humor. With a masterful control of language, Moyshe Leyb underlines his sense of alienation in the New World and his outrage at the poverty and injustice that surround him. Wandering at night, he creates hallucinatory scenes that fuse the cityscape with the nightscape of sea, moon and rock. His deft fusing of playfulness and melancholia make him one of a kind in Yiddish poetry. Y. Y. Schwartz (1885-1971) brings the epic into Yiddish with his touching and lyrical *Kentoki* (Kentucky), which captures the experience of Yiddish-speaking immigrants settling in "deep" America. The *Yunge* sought to explore the new land in which they found themselves, and *Kentoki* provides a sensitive picture of this experience. Also associated with *Di Yunge* was H. Leivick (1888-1962), perhaps the most esteemed American Yiddish poet. His work is fiercely ethical, providing ruminations on the suffering of mankind, Jewish martyrdom, and messianic hope. He was fascinated by Spinoza and wrote a number of philosophical poems about him. Leivick represents the consummate Yiddish poet, a man who was modern, questioning, caught by the tragic sense of life and Jewish life in particular; his verse bears the weight of the world and the thread of ethical determination in a society where justice is rare.

The *Yunge* drew together in their various anthologies a fine collection of poets who shared in the excitement of building a secular Jewish culture and a poetry that was modern but not yet modernist. Still, they felt the loneliness of exile and were not at home in America. How could they be? America had not conceived of a secular, active, non-English-speaking culture in its midst, and these Jewish poets were yet to find an audience in America outside of their Jewish confreres.

World War One destroyed all the accommodations Jews had made with the Tsarist authorities and with the Austrian-Hungarian Empire. Now the Jews, who for centuries had made a home in Eastern Europe – albeit with numerous restrictions placed upon them – found themselves increasingly alienated in their surroundings. In the new independent nation-states such as Poland, Romania, the Baltic States, and the Ukraine, the Jews were unwanted minorities with little security, although their minority rights were supposedly guaranteed by the League of Nations. The Bolshevik Revolution of 1917 further separated Jews from East Central Europe, and with the 1919 Civil War in Russia and the Ukraine, the misery and the horrific pogroms reached unprecedented levels.

The period following World War One, despite the intolerable conditions, would produce a flourishing of Yiddish poetry on the highest levels of aesthetic accomplishment. The Yiddish poets of this era participated in the literary and artistic avant-gardes and were fully abreast of European ideological and stylistic movements. Prior to World War One, Warsaw and Vilna had served as the traditional centers of Yiddish culture; after the war, three new centers of Yiddish culture and poetry rapidly emerged. In the new Soviet Union, the center was first Kiev (1918-1920), and then Moscow. In Poland, the focus was Lodz (1919), and then Warsaw after 1920. The third center was New York. These three centers were in contact during the first half of the '20s, but after the 1929 stock market crash and the closing up of the Soviet Union under Stalin, these communities became creative units of diminishing quality and production. Minor centers emerged as well, particularly in Romania, Paris, Buenos Aires and Johannesburg. The impact of collapsed economic realities, political and ideological differences, and distinct aesthetic visions created unhappy barriers, and, as fascism flourished, the Jews found themselves suffering as never before in diasporic history.

Immediately following the Russian Revolution, Kiev became the center for Yiddish creativity. Poets gathered around the *Kultur-Lige*, the national Yiddish secular-oriented center of educational and cultural activities, which had its own publishing house. Two modern poets from just before the war, Dovid Hofshteyn (1889-1952) and Leyb Kvitko (1893-1952), were joined by new poets, particularly Perets Markish (1895-1952) and Arn Kushnirov (1890-1949). Hofshteyn's verse uses spare language to express his amazement at the world about him. Elements of futurism are recognizable in his portrayal of city life, but his somewhat abstract treatment of nature creates a mood of quiet refinement. Leyb Kvitko's verse is more open to folkloric elements and he made use of his knowledge of Slavic culture to enrich his poetry with a fresh lyricism. But it is Markish who best represents the new age with his revolutionary romanticism. He embraces the New and the Revolution as a liberation reflected in his person. He explodes with delight at the world and its sensual presence – at least in his first sheaves. Markish and fellow poet Itsik Fefer (1900-1952) would become the two best examples of Bolshevik Yiddish poetry. The Kiev era was probably the happiest and most hopeful moment in Yiddish poetry in Europe. By 1921, the communist victory closed down the cultural autonomy of this Ukrainian hour, and Yiddish poets moved off to be replaced by a newer group of proletariat-oriented poets.

Around the same time in Lodz, Poland, Moshe Broderzon, fresh from Moscow, joined with local artists and poets to create *Yung-Yidish*, a journal dedicated to creating a new secular Jewish culture in Poland. The journal became a way to give voice to the expressionistic credo of the new age, and to try and make sense of a world gone mad. The publication lasted but one year, 1918, but established a new generation of poets and paved the way for the development of modern Yiddish poetry in the capital, Warsaw. The transitional journal *Ringen* (1921) brought together the Lodz poets with the new poets arriving in Warsaw. The new arrivals were determined that Warsaw, with its vast Yiddish-speaking population, should become the center of Yiddish culture in Europe. The key figures were the Bohemian *révoltés* Uri Zvi Greenberg (1896-1981), Melekh Ravitch (1893-1976) and, direct from Moscow, Perets Markish. They banded together and outraged the traditional world by having a poetry recital on Saturday (Sabbath) morning in a theater. Declared a *Khalyastre* (a "wild gang") by the leading critic and religious mystic Hillel Tseytlin, these poets "hijacked" the term as their coat-of-arms, using it for their movement and the title of their journal. This troika of poets was united in the desire to create a new culture and unique poetry, but each poet had his own perspective. Nonetheless, they agreed on a general statement: "Our measure is not beauty but horror." Their poetry was to destroy the old and welcome the new. Uri Zvi Greenberg, haunted by pogroms, sought an intense Jewish consciousness in his verse, using metaphors and imagery drawn from Kabbala and Khasidic writings. He raised the tone of his verse, peppering it with Hebrew and Aramaic words and phrases unique to the Jewish tradition and creating a prophetic tonality. "Thus the gruesome in the poem/thus the chaotic in the image/thus the outcry of the blood" (from "Albatros 3"). Melekh Ravitch, the youngest, sought a metaphysical tonality and sophisticated projection of worldiness and sensuality, with philosophical concerns. Perets Markish wrote some of his finest verse in Warsaw: *Di Kupe* (The Mound), a powerful expressionist dirge for the victims of the 1919 Civil War pogroms; *Radio*, a propagandistic work for Bolshevism and the laments of the poet in exile; and *Volin*, a highly descriptive vision of shtetl life rich in rare Yiddish local terminology. These poets went around the country declaiming their verse and exposing the youth to modernist poetry. By 1923, Greenberg, considered an undesirable in Poland, fled to Berlin to publish his journal *Albatros*, the most advanced journal of Yiddish poetry ever produced and the equal to most avant-garde art in Europe at the time. Markish went to Paris and published the *Khalyastre* there. Then he returned to Warsaw and joined with Ravitch and Israel Joshua Singer to publish *Literarishe Bleter* (Literary Pages; 1924), the most important literary journal in inter-war Poland. By 1926, the *Khalyastre* had broken up: Markish returned to the Soviet Union; Greenberg had abandoned Yiddish and Europe prophesizing the extermination of Jewry and fled to Tel Aviv to become a great Hebrew poet and ultra-nationalist; and Ravitch remained in Poland, supporting cultural autonomy, but saw the dreams of a new Yiddish culture unraveling until he fled to Australia and finally Canada.

The poetry scene in New York at the end of World War One was in ferment as a new generation of poets not much younger than *Di Yunge* emerged with all the intensity of the Jazz Age, announcing themselves as *In Zikhistn* (Introspectivists) and calling their journal *In Zikh* (*Within the Self*, 1920). They were determined to create poetry that was free of art-for-art's-sake decadence, and to write well-made verse that captured moods and minutiae. Poetry was to be made from fragments torn out of the self and proffered as reflections of one's inner life. It should not be linear and narrative but should have multiple perspectives, playing with the simultaneity of time and space. Their poetry was mainly in free verse, and experimental in its placement on the page and its use of rhythm. Verbal virtuosity and linguistic play opened poetry to new images and themes, while the notion of the poem as fragment permitted a concentration of imagery and an intensity of emotion. But their move towards modernism came at a time when their readership was shrinking: some Yiddish readers were alienated by their experiments in language and perspective, while others readers were lost to English-language literature. The poets felt their growing isolation and were discomforted.

These new poets were affected by imagism, vorticism and expressionism. They had a Western university experience – unlike the earlier poets – and spoke English fluently, but chose Yiddish, their mother tongue, as the instrument of their fullest identity. They did not feel compelled to treat identifiable Jewish themes or play the role of official "Jewish poets," but in their use of the language they revealed their love of Yiddish, and they underlined their pride as poets of Yiddish in their manifesto (1919). The key figures were Arn Glants-Leyeles (1889-1966), who, along with Nahum Barukh Minkoff (1893-1958), developed the group's theoretical position; and the most gifted, Jacob Glatstein (1896-1971). All three captured the urban life of New York and exploited new themes and imagery of the Machine Age. The subways rumble, Broadway bounces alive with people. The poet breathes at one with, and yet apart from his world. Glatstein takes the reader to the funeral of "Sheeny Mike," the Jewish gangster, or into a shop where a young cobbler shining shoes dreams like Sinbad in the torrent of city life. Glatstein could also carry one off to Biblical expansions or Khassidic memories, particularly as Europe fell dark and then the *Shoah* left him with only rehearsals of the past. He could curse too, and his "Good Night, World" made clear his scorn of Western hypocrisy and his embrace of his tattered Yiddish world, in much the same way that Aimé Césaire in the same years embraced his Négritude. The pain of watching his language and culture rent by human brutality and the insensitive flow of history provided his final verses of praise for his beloved instrument, Yiddish, at its last and most virtuoso hour. His death marked a passing of Yiddish poetry in America.

During the same post-World War One years as the *In Zikhistn*, the new Soviet Yiddish poetry sought to distinguish itself with verse that celebrated the new age, communism, the worker, and a farewell to the past shtetl lifestyle. In 1922 the 'fellow travelers' gathered around the Moscow journal *Shtrom* (Stream), and attempted to maintain a unity with the other Yiddish centers. The thrust of Soviet policies led to its demise in 1924, but in its short life, the journal permitted many new Soviet Yiddish poets to emerge. Itsik Fefer, in contrast, had little patience with the modernist tendencies of Markish and the fellow travelers; he wrote poems in *proste reyd* (down home talk) to reach the Yiddish-speaking masses. He conformed to Soviet wishes fully and celebrated all Soviet events in verse, supported the Birobidzhan project of a Soviet Jewish entity, and conformed willingly to the Soviet socialist realist literary policies of the government. Shmuel Halkin (1897-1960) was somewhat more canny in his Soviet art. Erudite and cautious, his early verse contrasted the melancholic attitudes of the present against the future fulfillment of communism. Izi Kharik (1898-1937) was initially praised for his long poem, *Minsker Blotes* (Minsk Marshes; 1924), which described the changes of a shtetl during the revolution. In his later verse, however, he revealed his ambivalence towards the notion of a fulfilled socialist world, and he paid for this ambivalence with his life in the Great Purges of 1937. The remarkable poet Moshe Kulbak (1896-1937), who elected to come to the Soviet Union from Vilna in 1928, also lost his life in the Purge. His poetry from 1916-1928 fused romantic nostalgia with a stylized folkishness that stressed modern themes, such as the city, the discovery of nature, a loving but ironic appreciation of rural Jews, and teasing allusions to traditional texts. His poem *Vilne* (Vilna) describes a culture of exilic Jerusalem that was sadly in decline. His sheaf of verse, *Raysn* (White Russia), wonderfully depicts the everyday life of the Jewish country folk. And in his long poem *Disner Childe-Harold*, Kulbak writes of a Lithuanian Jewish intellectual who is studying in Berlin, and uses this protagonist to highlight the complexities of modern life. The poem uses drama, lyricism, rich imagery, and juxtapositions of time and space to deliver the inevitable judgment of bourgeois decadence for a Soviet audience.

The Purges left Yiddish poets and writers adrift and wary. During the Second World War expressions of nationalistic fervor were tolerated, but by 1948 such activities were considered anti-Soviet, and many Yiddish poets, writers, and critics were arrested. On August 12, 1952, the poets Dovid Hofshteyn, Perets Markish, Itsik Fefer and Leyb Kvitko and many other poets and prose writers were put to death. All Yiddish publications were suppressed between 1949-1959, and afterwards only a handful of texts appeared yearly until the end of the Soviet Regime. Irving Howe summed up the Soviet Yiddish experience as "ashes out of hope."

In Romania during the '20s and '30s, Yiddish poetry made a remarkable contribution to the culture in the persons of Eleazer Shteynbarg (1880-1932), Yankev Shternberg and Itzik Manger (1901-1969). Shteynbarg produced lyric fables that rival the Russian fabulist Krylov, or at times France's La Fontaine. He utilized every register of the language, including bringing back archaic vocabulary and rare idioms, and he shaped his verse to carry every nuance of *Yiddishkayt*, the collective spirit of Eastern European Jewry drawn from both the folk and from the Bible, Talmud, Midrash and Rabbinic *Responsa*. Shteynbarg's ironic humor and didactic insights always side with the underdog. His art places him among the best poets Yiddish has ever produced, and his ironic fables are classics for the ages. Shternberg belongs to a lesser order but his enchantment with the modern city reveals the modernist even in Romania, and his verse eschews folkic effects as he attempts to proffer the rhythms of the modern age. Shteynbarg's only rival for virtuoso teasing with language, syntactical play, and quick wit inside traditional forms is Itzik Manger who, picking up Mani Leyb's love of ballads, constructs ballads of remarkable imagery and narrative bite, fusing fantasia and the grotesque with depths of shaded alienation. Itzik Manger came to Warsaw in the '30s and was beloved as the impish bohemian troubadour whose extraordinary retelling of the Esther story, the tales of the Bible reset in the Carpathian Mountains, and Bessarabia enchanted the Jewish community in those threatening days, providing a welcome retreat into traditional cultural references. Manger created an entire epic retelling of biblical tales in Eastern European garb of the late ninteenth century; after the Holocaust he collected this work in its final form as *Medresh Itsik* (Itsik's Midrash; 1951). The narrative of each retelling reveals a lyric ballad traversed with humor, but with an intense Jewish folkloric intimacy and sensibility. He survived the war and, after unhappy days in New York, died in Israel, singing his delight at coming home.

Jewish male poets were less than appreciative of their feminine counterparts, but the flowering of female poets brought a fresh and distinctive approach to artistic expression. Each one displays her own personality but shares a concern for clarity of expression and the candid treatment of themes, particularly sexual ones, that embarrassed their male counterparts. They were perhaps fifty years ahead of their time in terms of women's liberation. Miriam Ulinover (1890-1944) used Eastern European Jewish motifs to reveal, with wry humor, the tension between repetitions of tradition and the modern woman. Celia Dropkin (1887-1956) and Anna Margolin (1887-1952) both take up modern passion, sexual desire, their bodies and pleasure, and permit themselves to express scorn and even outrage at their husbands and lovers, especially for their insensitivity and ignorance. Dropkin uses directness with powerful, cutting intent, while Margolin employs the same rhetoric with a tighter control. Kadie Molodowsky (1894-1975) displays a lyrical toughness in her defense of beleaguered women and children in the '30s, but in post-war America, it was the theme of exile and memory that came to the fore. In her final years she lived in a small apartment with her lover and slept on a bed under which she kept piles of extra copies of her journal *Svive* (Milieu). Dvora Fogel (?-1943) was the first Yiddish poet to introduce cubist and surrealist elements into Yiddish verse. Her poems read like formal constructs, but her unexpected juxtapositions of imagery make her verses glow from within. She was once the lover of Bruno Schulz but was murdered with her husband and children in the Holocaust. Rokhl Korn (1898-1982) from Galicia created intense love poetry that was tied to the world of nature. She caught the tensions of village life between Jews and Gentiles just before World War Two, and then exposed the pain of exile in her new home in Montreal, Canada. Rajzel Zychlinsky (1910-) has been publishing poetry since 1936. Her work, much admired by Itsik Manger, is tight and spare, and hints at multiple and hidden mystical dimensions. All these female poets preferred to express themselves in a Yiddish that eschewed Hebraic or Slavic lexical elements, as if to make evident that they had no need to display their erudition, but rather wished to reveal their dominance of their instrument in its natural condition. The same can be said of their syntactical structures, which are closest to natural speech patterns. The women poets achieved a remarkable level of aesthetic success and intellectual penetration, and in their poetry have often employed more modern and modernist elements than their male counterparts.

Poland of the late '20s and '30s produced a plethora of Yiddish poets, most of whose lives would be cut short by the Holocaust. The majority were left-leaning and cosmopolitan, but there was a minority who leaned toward the inherited Jewish traditions: Arn Tseytlin (189-1973), Yisroel Shtern (1894-1943), and Khayim Semyatitski (1908-1943). They were either drawn to theological cosmic considerations, khassidic mysticism, or Jewish religious concerns. Their voices, though lyric, are generally dark, and a certain heaviness surrounds these souls as they search for liberation. Their verse reflects the uneasy Jew who is trying to use his cultural inheritance to create new meaning and beauty.

In the last years of the inter-war period, a new group of poets emerged in Poland called *Yung Vilne* (Young Vilna), of whom the best were Khayim Grade (1910-1982), Elkhonen Vogler (1907-1969), Leyzer Volf (1910-1943), and Abraham Sutzkever (1913-). They shared the sense of a traditional world in disarray, but their attachments range from Grade's deep appreciation of the Yiddish inheritance, to Volf and Vogler's sense of detachment, to Sutzkever's enthusiastic modernism. Today the poetry of Sutzkever is considered the finest of the *Yung Vilne* group. After the war he moved to Israel and established the last major journal of Yiddish literature, *Di Goldene Keyt* (The Golden Chain), which continued into the twenty-first century. From his childhood memories in *Sibir* (Siberia), to his most recent verses, through poetry written in the Vilna Ghetto to his mature years in Israel, Sutzkever reveals an immense command of the Yiddish instrument, bringing new moods, themes, tones, and linguistic play to the reader, and proving the vitality of the Yiddish language and culture, even as it appears to once again be approaching its demise. Sutzkever's poetry ranges from personal expression to an ekphrasis on a Chagall canvas. A strong surrealist bent runs through his lyric art, and his rhythms are new and unexpected. As Isaac Bashevis Singer is the last Yiddish master in prose, so, fearfully, it appears that Sutzkever is the last great poet in Yiddish. And yet their accomplishments continue in the Jewish literature written in Hebrew, English and other tongues and now used by Jews to express their existential realities.

In little more than one hundred years, Yiddish poetry, unknown as a discipline in 1875, produced a body of fine poets and poetry. This verse created and mirrored the image of a Jewish people turning the corner from tradition to modernity, and rendered, in their daily tongue, a body of work that is able to stand proud amidst the finest stars of twentieth century poetry. By embracing their own literature, the eastern European Jews discovered an unassailable, timeless territory of Mind, a space in which they could express their spiritual and psychological needs during a period of destabilization. Their hopes for cultural legitimacy may have dissolved in the inundations of physical hate, but their poetry joins other poetic inheritances of cultural catastrophe, voices extinguished before their time: their work lives on for all mankind to appreciate, encouraging us to reflect on what was, and what should have been.

– *Seth L. Wolitz*
  Gale Chair of Jewish Studies
  Professor of Comparative Literature
  University of Texas at Austin

WITH EVERYTHING WE'VE GOT

Yiddish Poets Speak to
Me from the Grave

Translate us,
as if you were returning
to your childhood,
as if you'd missed it
and now find it – a gift
age has given you.
Translate us,
as if you'd postponed
your own life,
and just now return to it,
happy to find
that nothing
can keep you from us.

When you go down,
when you visit us,
walk where you feared to go.
We will speak Yiddish,
our words shaking off
the darkness, and gathering
around you. We will
be patient.
Only now, Ruvn,
only now,
do you know
how long
we've been waiting
for you,
above and below.

1

Prokofiev's *Overture on Hebrew Themes*
(a lyric for Sheva)

Eerie clarinet-Jew quivers in the air,
Klarnetyidl tsaplt umheymlekh in aver,

his shadow thieves along the wall – a strain of *M.*
af der vant ganvet zikh zayn shotn – a ton fun Mem.

He despoils notes and measures and scales.
Notn un taktn fardreyt er, tener un games.

Prokofiev hears rifts in him.
Prokofyev hert shpaltungen in im.

Tense licks pucker, whine,
Geshpante lekn kneytshn zikh un yomern,

like a sexual whimper dying out, going on.
vi a seksuel vimpernish vos geyt oys un geyt on.

Jew seeps from all instruments, not just the fiddle.
Nit nor funem fidl, nor fun ale keylim krikht aroys dos yidl.

His sounds invest the air we breathe in,
Zayne klangen nemen iber di luft vos mir otemen,

alter blood driving to the heart, regress to jokes.
makhn iber blut vos loyft tsum harts, geyen arop tsu khokhmes.

Plaintive, flouting Jew penetrating the notes, Prokofiev hears him.
In di notn hert Prokofyev dos yidl, vu er dringt arayn.

RICHARD J. FEIN

Tkhine on Operating a Stall in the Marketplace

Ever-present God,
my heart is as heavy as the buckets
on the shoulders of water carriers,
my mind as dark
as the backs of horses in the marketplace –
more sellers than buyers.
Ever-present God,
I want to be honest,
neither lie nor cheat,
for I know
You see me
huddling near the firepan
by my bin of wrinkled apples.
Every kopeck is dear to me,
my heart claps amazed
how my tongue barks for the sale.

Ever-present God,
help me with Your firm hand,
the same hand that guided Rachel
as she gathered her wares.
Dear, dear God,
the money is little, the pain great.

Ever-present God,
I haven't time for all Your prayers.
Sunset comes
and I should be home for *shabbes*.

3

The well-to-do Jews are already bathed,
their candles glow in their candlesticks.
By the time I get home
my husband has lit the candles –
that deed You granted women –
but my fingers snuff out the lights.
Then three sins weigh on my conscience –
I am late for *shabbes*,
I curse my husband for lighting the candles,
I pinch them and light them again.
O dear, dear God,
look at what I am –
a woman who ruins *shabbes*
with her quarrels and her curses.

God – An Ear

(after Yehoash's Yiddish translation of the 102nd Psalm)

God – an ear.
My life wears out –
like twines of cigarette smoke.
I have fever.
My bones stare like an X-ray.
My flesh is like grass in August.
I'm a sparrow in a city gutter.
I'm an owl on an unhinged gate.
I'm a crow on a charred beam.
My enemies circle me.
I remember to eat, sometimes –
the bread is dry,
the coffee oily and bitter.

It's time – show some pity –
You who made all.
Your name fixes us.
You built Zion.
You hear the dispersed.
You move beyond scorn.

I am tired,
but please don't cut my days;
less than half are left.
You – You count differently.
Once upon a time you parceled light, made days,
    crafted heaven.
Yet they too wear out –
cash clothes for the rag man.
You will return to pre-light, pre-days –
before you gathered and crafted.
You keep beyond the worlds
You made.

5

Mani Leyb

(1883 - 1953)

A Plum

In the cool evening the owner
pulled a ripe plum from the tree
and with it a leaf.
He bit into the dewy

blue skin and the slumbrous juice
burst coolly into his grip. To keep
the full juiciness – and not lose a drop –
he slowly carried it, the way one

cradles a cup of wine in both
hands, and gently lifted it
to his wife's lips. Lovingly, she

thanked him and gnawed
the plum in his hands down
to skin and pit and speckled pulp.

מאַני לייב

(1953 - 1883)

אַ פֿלוים

אין קילן אָוונט האָט דער בעל-הבית
פֿון בוים אַ רײַפֿן פֿלוים אַראָפּגעריסן
אין איינעם מיטן בלאַט, און אײַנגעביסן
די טרייַק בלויע הויט. האָט פֿון זײַן שלאָס

דער שלאָפֿעדיקער זאַפֿט געטאָן אַ גאָס
מיט קילן שוים. און צו פֿאַרשליסן
איר גאַנצן זאַפֿט - אַ טראָפּן ניט פֿאַרגיסן -
האָט ער פֿאַמעלעך, ווי מען טראָגט אַ כּוס

מיט ווײַן, אין בײַדע פֿולע הענט די פֿלוים
געבראַכט דער ווײַב און אײדל צוגעטראָגן
צו אירע ליפּן. האָט זי מיט אַ ליבן

„אַ דאַנק" - פֿון זײַנע הענט גענומען נאָגן
די פֿלוים. ביז אין די הענט איז אים פֿאַרבליבן
די הויט, דאָס בײַנדל און צעקלעקטער שוים.

7

Plums in Winter

"Mmm really tasty," I say aloud
while munching on a plum from Chile.
You watch and ask, "Can I have a bite?"
"No… get your own." Then suddenly
Mani Leyb's "A Plum" comes to mind –
the man who shares his plum with his wife –
Why, I've even translated it! Read the Yiddish
to residents at a nursing home, hoping they'd get it!
And now, abashed, I reach across and hand
you the plum, "Here, take all you want."
You take a healthy bite and hand me
back the rest, "Here, finish it," and
I taste the rest of the skin, the pulp, the juice,
and this slithery pit that's still in my mouth.

Moyshe-Leyb Halpern
(1886 - 1932)

Zlotshev, My Home

Oh Zlotshev, my home, my town,
With your steeple, shul, and bathhouse.
With your women of the marketplace,
With your little Jews who scurry
Like dogs after the peasant carrying
His basket of eggs from Sasover Mountain –
Like springtime, my life awakens in me
My poor, little yearning for you –
My home, my Zlotshev.

While yearning, I also recall
Rappaport the rich man carrying
His prominent belly to shul,
And Shaye Hillel, the pious bigot,
Who would even sell the sunshine
Like a pig in a sack –
That's enough to extinguish in me,
Like a candle, my longing for you –
My home, my Zlotshev.

משה־לייב האַלפּערן

(1932 - 1886)

זלאָטשעוו, מײַן היים

אַ זלאָטשעוו, דו, מײַן היים, מײַן שטאָט
מיט דײַן קלויסטערשפּיץ און שול און באָד.
און מיט דײַנע זיצערקעס אויפֿן מאַרק
און מיט דײַנע ייִדלעך וואָס רײַסן זיך אָפּ
ווי הינט אויף דעם פּויער וואָס קומט אַראָפּ
מיט אַ קוישל אייער פֿון סאַסאָווער באַרג -
ווי דאָס לעבן אין פֿרילינג וואַכט אויף אין מיר
מײַן אָרעם ביסל בענקשאַפֿט צו דיר, -
מײַן היים, מײַן זלאָטשעוו.

נאָר אַז איך דערמאָן זיך פֿאַרבענקטערהייט
אָן דעם נגיד ראַפּעפאָרט, ווי ער גייט
מיט זײַן גראָבן בויך אין שול אַרײַן,
און אָן שיִע הללס, דעם פֿרומאַק,
וואָס וואָלט ווי אַ חזיר אין אַ זאַק
פֿאַרקויפֿט אַפֿילו די זון מיט איר שײַן -
איז דאָס גענוג, עס זאָל אויסגיין אין מיר,
אַזוי ווי אַ ליכט, מײַן בענקשאַפֿט צו דיר, -
מײַן היים, מײַן זלאָטשעוו.

How does the story go about that dandy:
How once at dusk he saw
An endless stream of angels around the sun,
Until a goy, a drunk with an axe,
Gave him such a blow through his vest
That it almost killed him –
That goy with the axe is the hate in me
For my grandfather and for you –
My home, my Zlotshev.

Your earth knows I'm not inventing:
When my grandfather called the police
To throw my mother out of the house,
My grandmother stood with her legs apart,
Smiling almost sweetly as honey,
Like a shiksa between two soldiers –
I curse the hate in me,
Reminding me of her and of you –
My home, my Zlotshev.

Like a bunch of naked Jews
Surrounding a scalded man in the bathhouse,
Onlookers rocked and petted their beards
Around the tossed-out packs,
The rags and tatters in bundles,
And around the pieces of a poor bed –
My mother still cries in me,
Just as she did under your sky, in you –
My home, my Zlotshev.

ווי דערצײילט זיך די מעשה פֿון יענעם פֿראָנט:
ער האָט אײן מאָל פֿאַר נאַכט אזוי לאַנג נאָך אנאַנד
געזען מלאכים אַרום דער זון,
ביז סע האָט אים א שיכּור, א גוי מיט א האַק
אַזאַ מין פֿאַרפֿאָר געטאָן אונטערן פֿראַק,
אַז ר׳איז נעבעך שיער נישט געשטאָרבן דערפֿון –
דער גוי מיט דער האַק איז מײַן שׂינאה אין מיר
צו מײַן זײידן, און אים צו ליב אויך צו דיר, –
מײַן היים, מײַן זלאָטשעוו.

דײַן ערד איז אַן עדות, אַז איך טראַכט נישט אויס.
ווען מײַן זײידע האָט מײַן מאַמען פֿון הויז
אַרויסגעשטעלט מיט דער פֿאָליציי,
האָט מײַן באָבע אין דער ברײט מיט די פֿיס
געשמײכלט שיער אַזוי האָניק זיס,
ווי אַ שיקסע וואָס שטײט צווישן זעלנער צוויי –
אַז פֿאַרשאָלטן זאָל ווערן מײַן שׂינאה אין מיר,
וואָס האָט מיך דערמאָנט אָן איר און אָן דיר, –
מײַן היים, מײַן זלאָטשעוו.

ווי אַ קופּקעלע נאַקעטע יידן אין באָד
אַרום אַ פֿאַרבריטן, האָט מען אין ראָד
געשאָקלט די קעפּ און די בערד זיך געגלעט
אַרום די אַרויסגעוואָרפֿענע פּעק
און שמאַטעס און בעבעכעס אין זעק
און אַרום דעם צעבראָקענעם שטיקל בעט –
מײַן מאַמע ווײַנט נאָך איצטער אין מיר,
ווי דעמאָלט אונטער דײַן הימל אין דיר, –
מײַן היים, מײַן זלאָטשעוו.

13

Yet marvelous is our world:
Crossing a field with a horse and wagon,
You drag yourself to the train,
Which tears like a demon over fields,
Depositing you into steerage;
You're borne over water to downtown New York –
And that really is my only comfort,
That they won't bury me in you –
My home, my Zlotshev.

נאָר װוּנדערלעך איז דאָך אונדזער װעלט.

מיט אַ פֿערד און װאָגן איבער אַ פֿעלד

שלעפּט מען זיך אַרױס צו דער באַן,

װאָס פֿליט װי אַ שד איבער פֿעלדער אַװעק,

ביז זי ברענגט אױף אַ שיף מיט אַ צװישנדעק,

װאָס פֿירט אַריבער קײן ניו־יאָרק דאָונטאָון, –

איז דאָס טאַקע די אײנציקע טרײסט כּאָטש פֿאַר מיר,

װאָס מען װעט מיך נישט באַגראָבן אין דיר, –

מײַן הײם, מײַן זלאָטשעװ.

Evening

He's often seen these boulders on the beach.
I've wondered, what draws a man of my age
here, to the beach, in the autumn dusk?
What is it about the smoke that rises from ships,
about the cloud disappearing on the western edge of the sky?
When a child begins Hebrew school he is taught
to say a blessing over the piece of bread he holds in his hand.
But who teaches a man of my age to go around alone
and groan at the fog that settles into night?
At the wind that cries like himself?
At the white crests of waves, always dancing their death-dance?
O, Gingili, you, my mood-swings –
like rust that spreads over an old sword,
loneliness embraces my limbs;
and like a dying bird that leaves its nest,
night falls over me.
I never stop talking to myself about these things,
just as some holy fool talks to the wind by an open window,
to the wind that blows out the light near a sacred book.

אָוונט

איך האָב געטראַכט –

– אַ מאַן אין מײנע יאָרן,

וואָס ציט אים דאָ אַהער צום ים אין האַרבסטיקן פֿאַרנאַכט?

די שטיינער דאָ האָט ער דאָך שוין געזען

און וואָס איז אים דער רויך, וואָס ציט זיך פֿון אַ שיפֿסקוימען אַרויף?

און וואָס איז אים דער וואָלקן, וואָס פֿאַרשווינדט

בײם מערבֿ־זוים פֿון הימל?

אַ קינד הייבט אָן אין חדר גיין,

לערנט מען אים אויס ברכה מאַכן

אויף דעם שטיקל ברויט אין העניל, וואָס ער האַלט.

ווער אָבער לערנט אויס אַ מענטש אין מײנע יאָרן

אַרומצוגיין אַליין

און זיך קלאָגן וועגן דעם

צום נעפֿל, וואָס ער זעט אין רוים אין דעם נאַכטיקן?

צום ווינט, וואָס ווײנט ווי ער?

און צו דעם ווײסן שוים, וואָס טאַנצט פֿון ים אַרויס

זײן אייביקן טויטנטאַנץ?

אָ, גינגעלי, מײן אומרו דו –

ווי זשאַווער אויף אַ שווערד אַן אַלטער

לינט די אײנזאַמקייט אויף מײנע גלידער;

און ווי פֿון נעסט אַרויס אַ פֿויגל, וואָס איז קראַנק צום שטאַרבן,

פֿאַלט אויף מיר די נאַכט.

און אייביק רעד איך וועגן דעם צו זיך אַליין,

ווי עס רעדט אַ נאַר אַ הייליקער צום ווינט בײם אָפֿענעם פֿענצטער,

צום ווינט, וואָס האָט בײם ים דאָס ספֿר אים דאָס ליכט פֿאַרלאָשן.

17

In the World

Who has grasped the hunger-song
the wolf sings on the white steppe at night?
Like a star close to the white earth,
a small fire mourns, off in the distance,
where the wolf, with his throat and eyes, like blood,
sings his hunger-song on the steppe.
And Chaim is not the name of the wolf in the world,
and Stepan is not the name of the wolf in the world,
and he doesn't have a warm home in the world,
just the hair standing up on his skin
under the blood and gold of the moon,
and the white emptiness at the core of the world
surrounds him like a yellow sea –
and his limbs yearn to plunder,
like a dying man seeking light in the darkness. –
And white as his white teeth,
his breath steams out of him, mournful
under the blood and gold of the moon –
And Jesus didn't look any different
when he walked on the waves of the sea
under the blood and gold of the moon,
his eyes strained toward heaven
as he stood there – all alone.

1924

אין דער וועלט

ווער האָט שוין פֿאַרנומען דאָס הונגערליד,
וואָס דער וואָלף זינגט, אין ווײַסן סטעפּ, בײַ נאַכט?
ווי אַ שטערן נאָענט פֿון דער ווײַסער ערד,
ווײַנט אַ פֿײַערל ערגעץ אין דער ווײַט,
און אַהין מיטן האַלדז און מיט אויגן, ווי בלוט,
זינגט דער וואָלף אין סטעפּ זײַן הונגערליד.

און נישט חיים הייסט דער וואָלף אין דער וועלט;
און נישט סטעפֿאַן הייסט דער וואָלף אין דער וועלט
און ער האָט נישט קיין וואָרעמע היים אין דער וועלט, –
בלויז די אויפֿגעשטעלטע האָר אויף זײַן פֿעל
בײַ דער שײַן פֿון לבֿנהס בלוטיקן גאָלד
און אַזוי ווי אַ גאָלדענער ים זעט אויס אַרום אים
די ווײַסע פּוסטקייט אין מיטן דער וועלט – – –
און די גלידער זײַנע בענקען נאָך רויב,
ווי אַ שטאָרבנדיקער נאָך ליכט אין דער פֿינצטער. – – –
און ווײַס ווי זײַנע ווײַסע צײן,
ווײַנט דער אָטעם, וואָס פֿאָרעט פֿון אים אַרויס
בײַ דער לבֿנהס בלוטיקן גאָלד. – – –
און יעזוס האָט דאָך נישט אויסגעזען אַנדערש,
ווען ער איז אויף די וואַלן פֿון ים
בײַ דער לבֿנהס בלוטיקן גאָלד
מיט אויגן, צום הימל, אַרויפֿגעשטרעקטע
געשטאַנען – איינער אַליין.

1924

Considering the Bleakness

Considering the bleakness
and the hoarse animal roar,
you would think it a desert
where a sick, old lion
crawls around a rock,
looking for a place
to lie down and die.
In truth, it was a vacant city
where a madman, on all fours,
was crawling around,
circling a collapsed house,
dragging from behind
a skull on a rope
tied to his belt.

לויט דער וויסטעניש

לויט דער וויסטעניש
און לויט דעם הייזעריקן חיישן געברום
האָט זיך געדאַכט, אַז ס׳איז אַ מידבר דאָרט
און אַז עס קריכט אַן אַלטער לייב
ארום אַ פֿעלדז ארום, ווייל ער איז קראַנק
און ווייל ער זוכט אַן אָרט
צו קענען זיך אַנידערלייגן שטאַרבן.
נאָר אין דער אמתן איז דאָס געווען אַ פּוסטע שטאָט
מיט אַ משוגענעם, וואָס איז אויף העֵנט און פֿיס
ארומגעקראָכן אין אַ ראָד
ארום אַ הויז אַן אײַנגעפֿאַלענעם.
און דאָס, וואָס האָט זיך נאָכגעשלעפּט פֿון הינטער אים,
איז בלויז געווען אַ שאַרבן אויף אַ שטריק
צום גאַרטל זײַנעם הינטן צוגעבונדן.

21

Yeats into Yiddish

‏"די זאַכן פֿאַלן זיך פֿונאַנדער, דער צענטער קאָן ניט האַלטן,
‏נאָלע הפֿקר צעלאָזט זיך אויף דער וועלט,
‏דאָס בלוטנעפֿלייץ צעלאָזט זיך, און אומעטום
‏די אומשולד־צערעמאָניע ווערט דערטרונקען..."

"[Things fall apart]...*der tsenter ken nit haltn...*"
Skimming the *Forverts*, I brake
for these italics – Yeats's vexation and vision
twitch in the Yiddish letters, which,
in my chronic struggle to grasp them, seem
restless, never thoroughly yielding
meaning but subsisting
in their own flourish, in
their own tremor. That quiver
of agitation in the Yiddish lettering
brings me closer to Yeats's mantic specters,
at the same time that fitful refusal
of the Yiddish letters to stay in place
predicates their power
to shift Yeats's scene from Irish wars and
Europe's carnage-births, and to conjure
pogromized Jews of the Ukraine.

You, My Restlessness

Who can look at the beauty of an ocean?
Who can look into the light of your eyes?
And not feel his heart torn from joy.
And not feel his heart torn from sorrow –
you, my restlessness. You.

Why do I long for you? Oh, tell me.
Not a single night goes by, a single day,
when I don't think of you, dream of you,
of you, you my life, you the heart of me –
you, my restlessness. You.

משה־לייב האלפערן

אומרו מײנע

ווער קען די שײנקײט פֿון אַ ים פֿאַרשטײן?
ווער קען די שײן פֿון דײנע אויגן זען?
און ניט צעריסן ווערן זאָל זײן האַרץ פֿאַר פֿרײד.
און ניט צעריסן ווערן זאָל זײן האַרץ פֿאַר לײד,
דו, אומרו מײנע, דו.

פֿאַר וואָס בענק איך אזוי נאָך דיר, אָ זאָג,
עס גייט דאָך ניט אַוועק אַ נאַכט, אַ טאָג,
און נאָר איך טראַכט פֿון דיר, און נאָר איך טרוים פֿון דיר –
פֿון דיר, פֿון דיר. דו לעבן מײנס, דו האַרץ אין מיר,
דו, אומרו מײנע, דו.

Anna Margolin

(1887 - 1952)

My Tribe Speaks

My tribe:

    Men in satin and velvet,

    long faces of pale silk,

    lips – entranced, glowing like coal;

    their hands caressing yellowed tomes.

    Deep in the night they talk to God.

    Merchants from Leipsk and Dansk.

    Gleaming cuffs. Elegant cigar smoke.

    Gemorah witticisms. German civilities.

    Glances shrewd and opaque,

    shrewd and sated.

    Don Juans, dealers, and seekers of God.

    A drunk;

    some apostates in Kiev.

My tribe:

    Women, like idols garnished with jewels,

    turning garnet from Turkish shawls,

    from the dark pleats of satin-de Lyons.

    The flesh is a sobbing willow,

אַנאַ מאַרגאָלין

(1952 - 1887)

מײַן שטאַם רעדט

מײַן שטאַם:

מענער אין אַטלעס און סאַמעט,

פּנימער לאַנג און בלייך זײַדן,

פֿאַרחלשטע גלוטיקע ליפֿן.

די דינע הענט צערטלען פֿאַרגעלטע פֿאָליאַנטן.

זיי רעדן אין טיפֿער נאַכט מיט גאָט.

און סוחרים פֿון לײַפּסק און פֿון דאַנסק.

בלאַנקע מאַנקעטן. איידעלער סיגאַרן־רויך.

גמרא־וויצן. דײַטשע העפֿלעכקייטן.

דער בליק איז קלוג און מאַט,

קלוג און איבערזאַט.

דאָן־זשואַנען, העגדלער און זוכער פֿון גאָט.

אַ שיכּור,

אַ פּאָר משומדים אין קיעוו.

מײַן שטאַם:

פֿרויען ווי געצן באַצירט מיט בריליאַנטן,

פֿאַרטונקלט רויט פֿון טערקישע טיכער,

שווערע פֿאַלדן פֿון סאַטין־דע־ליאָן.

אָבער דאָס לײַב איז אַ ווינענדיקע ווערבע,

27

fingers lie in the lap, like dry flowers,
and in the fading, veiled eyes
dead desire.

Grande-damen in calico and linen,
broad-boned and strong, making their moves
with cynical light laughter,
with calm speech and uncanny silence.
At dusk by the window of a poor house
they appear like statues,
and in their twilight eyes shudder
savage desires.

A man and a wife
I'm ashamed to talk about.

All of them – my tribe,
blood of my blood,
flame of my flame,
the dead and the living mixed;
sad, grotesque, large,
they tramp through me as through a dark house,
tramp with prayers and curses and laments.
They shake my heart like a copper bell,
my tongue quivering.
I don't recognize my own voice –
my tribe speaks.

אָבער ווי טרוקענע בלומען די פֿינגער אין שויס,
און אין די וועלקע פֿאַרשלייערטע אויגן
טויטע לוסט.

און גראָנד־דאַמען אין ציץ און אין ליווענט,
ברייטבייניק און שטאַרק, און באַוועגלעך,
מיטן פֿאַראַכטלעכן לייכטן געלעכטער,
מיט רויִקע רייד און אומהיימלעכן שווייגן.
פֿאַר נאַכט ביים פֿענצטער פֿון אָרעמען הויז
וואַקסן זיי ווי סטאַטוען אויס.
און עס צוקט דורך די דעמערנדע אויגן
גרויזאַמע לוסט.

און אַ פֿאָר,
מיט וועלכע איך שעם זיך.

זיי אַלע, מײַן שטאַם,
בלוט פֿון מײַן בלוט
און פֿלאַם פֿון מײַן פֿלאַם,
טויט און לעבעדיק אויסגעמישט,
טרויעריק, גראָטעסק און גרויס
טראַמפּלען דורך מיר ווי דורך אַ טונקל הויז.
טראַמפּלען מיט תּפֿילות און קללות און קלאַנג,
טרייסלען מײַן האַרץ ווי אַ קופּערנעם גלאָק,
עס וואַרפֿט זיך מײַן צונג,
איך דערקען ניט מײַן קול –
מײַן שטאַם רעדט.

29

When I Was in My Teens

When I was in my teens
I heard Socrates in the Agora.
My bosom friend, my lover,
had the most gorgeous chest in Athens.

Then, what a shining world of marble
Caesar made, I the last one left,
and my proud sister
was chosen to be my wife.

Crowned with roses, drinking into the night,
flushed and cozy, I heard
about that wimp from Nazareth
and wild stories about the Jews.

איך בין געווען אַ מאָל אַ ייִנגלינג

איך בין געווען אַ מאָל אַ ייִנגלינג,
געהערט אין פּאַרטיקאָס סאָקראַטן,
עס האָט מײַן בוזעמפֿרײַנד, מײַן ליבלינג,
געהאַט דעם שענסטן טאָרס אין אַטען.

געווען צעזאַר. און אַ העלע וועלט
געבויט פֿון מאַרמאָר, איך דער לעצטער,
און פֿאַר אַ ווײַב מיר אויסדערוויילט
מײַן שטאָלצע שוועסטער.

אין רויזנקראַנץ בײַם ים וויין ביז שפּעט
געהערט אין הויכמוטיקן פֿרידן
וועגן שוואַכלינג פֿון נאַזאַרעט
און ווילדע מעשׂיות וועגן ייִדן.

31

Filled with Night and Pain

Silence – sudden and deep
between the both of us,
like a confused letter
with omens of parting.
Like a sinking ship.

Silence – not a look, not a touch,
filled with night and pain
between the two of us,
as if we alone
close the door
to the Garden.

פֿול מיט נאַכט און געוויין

אַ שווײַגן פּלוצעם און טיף
צווישן אונדז בײדן,
ווי אַ צעטומלטער בריוו
מיטן אָנזאָג פֿון שײדן.
ווי אַ זינקענדע שיף.

אַ שווײַגן אָן אַ בליק, אָן אַ ריר,
פֿול מיט נאַכט און געוויין
צווישן אונדז בײדן,
ווי מיר וואָלטן אַלײן
צו אַ גן־עדן
פֿאַרשליסן די טיר.

33

She with the Cold, Marble Breasts

She with the cold, marble
breasts and slender hands
filled with light squandered
her beauty on garbage, on nothing.

Maybe that's what she wanted,
wanted unhappiness, the seven knives
of pain, wanted her life's blood
poured into garbage, into nothing.

Here she lies, broken and alone.
All shame has left her body.
Passerby – look, have pity,
and say nothing.

זי מיט די קאַלטע מאַרמאָרנע בריסט

זי מיט די קאַלטע מאַרמאָרנע בריסט
און מיט די שמאָלע ליכטיקע הענט,
זי האָט איר שײנקײט פֿאַרשװענדט
אויף מיסט, אויף גאָרנישט.

זי האָט עס אפֿשר געװאָלט, אפֿשר געגלוסט
צו אומגליק, צו זיבן מעסערס פֿון פײַן
און פֿאַרגאָסן דעם לעבנס הײליקן װײַן
אויף מיסט, אויף גאָרנישט.

איצט ליגט זי מיט אַ צעבראָכן געזיכט.
דער געשענדטער גײַסט פֿאַרלאָזט די שטײַג.
פֿאַרבײַגײער, האָב רחמנות און שװײַג –
זאָג גאָרנישט.

H. Leivick

(1888 - 1962)

Yiddish Poets

When I think about us – Yiddish poets –
all that I feel is despair;
I want to cry to myself, to plead –
and suddenly all my words are mute.

How strange our poems seem –
like ears of corn eaten by locusts;
one consolation – to be sick of ourselves
and steal about God's earth, like migrant guests.

The blood of our word on cold fingers,
from fingers to even colder sidewalks.
Poet – you cut a ridiculous figure, displaced,
ashamed, pacing your four walls.

Even when some neighbor, someone we know,
comes up from a cellar or down from a loft –
he hears in us some dumb voice of himself,
some solemnity to steer clear of.

ה. לייוויק

(1962 - 1888)

ייִדישע פּאָעטן

אַז איך טראַכט וועגן אונדז – ייִדישע פּאָעטן,
אַזאַ צער כאַפּט מיך אַ מאָל אַרום:
עס ווילט זיך שרײַבן צו זיך אַליין, בעטן, –
און דעמאָלט גראָד ווערן ווערטער שטום.

אַזוי משונהדיק זעען אויס אונדזערע לידער, –
ווי זאַנגען, וואָס אַ הײשעריק צעפֿרעסט;
אַ טרייסט: – צו ווערן זיך אַליין דערווידער,
צו שלײַכן זיך אויף גאָטס ערד, ווי פֿרעמדע געסט!

דאָס בלוט פֿון אונדזער ווארט אויף קאַלטע פֿינגער,
פֿון פֿינגער – אויף נאָך קעלטערן צעמענט;
אַ, פֿאַרשעמטע, לעכערלעכע זינגער,
פֿאַרדרוקטע אין פֿאַרשעמטערע פֿיר ווענט!

און אַז עס קומט אַן אייגענער, אַ נאָענטער
פֿון אַ קעלער, צי פֿון אַ שאָפּ אַרויס, –
זײַן שטומע צונג נאָר אין אונדז דערקאָנט ער,
און אונדזער פֿײַערלעכקייט מײַדט ער אויס.

37

And we are like childish, self-absorbed
knights, like Don Quixote, heated up by our
own excesses, trapped in fits and starts,
isolated freelancers of word and letter.

Sometimes, like provoked and nervous cats
who snatch their bewildered kittens from danger,
we grab the scruff of our poems by our teeth
and scurry through the streets of New York.

When I think about us – Yiddish poets –
all that I feel is despair;
I want to cry to someone near, to plead –
and suddenly all my words are mute.

און מיר, ווי קינדישע, פֿאַרליבטע ריטער,
ווי דאָן קיכאָט, מיט איבערכאַפֿטער מאָס,
מיר בלײַבן ציטערן מיט אונדזער ציטער,
אין עלנט, איבער יעדן וואָרט און אות.

און אַ מאָל, ווי קעץ מיט אויפֿגערייצטע גלידער
שלעפֿן זייערע קעצלעך פֿאַרווירט פֿון זאָרג, –
אַזוי שלעפֿן מיר פֿאַרן האַלדז אונדזערע לידער
צווישן די צײַן, איבער גאַסן פֿון ניו־יאָרק.

אַז איך טראַכט וועגן אונדז, ייִדישע פּאָעטן,
אַזאַ צער נעמט מיך אַ מאָל אַרום,
און עס ווילט זיך שרײַען צום נאָענטן, בעטן, –
און דעמאָלט גראָד ווערן ווערטער שטום.

With Everything We've Got

My friend said to me, "We Yiddish poets
should write our last poem and throw
it into a coffin, then, like pallbearers,
carry it through the Jewish neighborhoods.

We'll wrap our poems in blue cloth,
or maybe cover them in plain white,
like the white pages of our books,
which rot in cellars – food for mice.

Or cover them in red crepe, in memory
of poets sentenced to prisons and gulags
or exterminated by the hygienic visions
of a despot, Cain dressed in lederhosen.

Even those who've only written a single line
can carry the pine box in our procession
through the Jewish streets, as we wind our way
past stores and apartments, schoolyards, alleys.

The youngest poet will lead us; he'll unscrew
his fountain pen, hurl cap, barrel, clip
and point into the gutter. Then we'll do the same,
from East Broadway to the Brooklyn Bridge.

ה. לייוויק

התלהבותדיק, מיט העכסטן ברען

א חבֿר-דיכטער האָט גערעדט צו מיר אזוי צו זאָגן:
מיר זאָלן אַלע אָנשרײַבן דאָס לעצטע ליד.
דאָס ליד אַרײַנטאָן אין אַן אָרון און עס טראָגן
דורך גאַסן וווּ עס וווינט דער אַמעריקאַנער ייִד.

מיר וועלן אײַנהילן דאָס ליד אין בלויע טיכער,
און אפֿשר נאָר עס אײַנוויקלען אין פּראָסטן ווײַס,
אין בלעטערווײַס פֿון אַלע דיכטערס ביכער,
וואָס ליגן אין די קעלערן – אַ שפּײַז פֿאַר מײַז.

און אויך אין בלעטעררײַט פֿון אָפּגעראַמטע דיכטער,
וואָס וואָלגערן זיך אין תּפֿיסות, צי בײַם צפֿון-ים,
צי אפֿשר שוין געטייטע צו דער גלאָריע פֿון פֿאַרניכטער,
צו נוץ פֿון יעדן קיין וואָס פֿאַרשטעלט זיך פֿאַר אַ תּם.

און ווער עס האָט נאָר ווען אַ שורה-ליד געשריבן
וועט אונטערהייבן דעם פֿאַרדעקטן אָרון מיט זײַן האַנט,
דערנאָך, דורך גאַסן פֿאַר פּראָצעסיעס צונעקליבן,
מיט שטאָלצקייט לאָזן זיך צום ענדעברעג פֿון לאַנד.

פֿאָרויס וועט גיין דער ייִנגסטער, אין זײַן האַנט זײַן פֿעדער,
מיט פֿײַערלעכקייט וועט ער זי צעשמעטערן אויף שטיק,
אַ שלײַדער צום אַספֿאַלט, און גלײַך נאָך אים אַיעדער, –
אַזאַ אַ מאַרש פֿון איסט בראָדווי צו ברוקלין-בריק.

41

From the Bridge to Brownsville, to Flatbush,
to Brighton Beach, to Coney Island, Sea Gate,
and the Atlantic. We'll cast away our last poems –
the water coming in, the water going out.

We'll stand at the edge of the ocean
and look at the waves foaming in anger
or in praise of poets who with their own
hands fling their last gifts into the abyss.

And then what? – Then, we'll take the subway
back to our rooms, unhood our typewriters.
On those round, silvered keys, we'll write
an elegy – and give it everything we've got."

פֿון בריק - צו בראָנזוויל, און צו פֿלעטבוש, און צו בריטן,
צו קוני־איַילענד, און צו סי־גייט - צום אַטלאַנטיק־ים,
און אין די וויסע כוואַליעס, העט צו אַלע וויַיטן,
אַריַינוואַרפֿן אין שטורעם־ווירבל אונדזער לעצטן גראַם.

מיר וועלן אַלע שטיין דערנאָך ביַים ברעג אַטלאַנטיק,
און קוקן ווי די כוואַליעס טורעמען אין שוים,
אין צאָרן, צי אין לויב, וואָס דיכטער האָבן אייגנהאַנטיק
אַוועקגעשענקט דעם תהום דאָס פֿלאַטערניש פֿון זייער טרוים.

און נאָך דעם? - נאָך דעם וועלן מיר, צום טרוים געטריַיע,
צעשיידן זיך און אויסזוכן אַ ברוכשפּיץ פֿון אַ פּען,
און אָנשריַיבן אַ ניַי געזאַנג - אַ קינה־ליד אויף דער לוויה
און אָנשריַיבן דאָס ליד התלהבותדיק, מיט העכסטן ברען!

43

A Yiddish Poet
Thinks of His Readers

The unhappy few in New York.
Their speech passed on.
No more cursing, gossiping,
joking, selling, yelling on the street,
voices like fishes flitting into my net.
My potential readers
readers of Eliot,
perhaps taking the long way around
to come back to me
for the first time,
like that jazz musician who played
Brazilian and Cuban melodies,
returning at seventy to klezmer sounds
of childhood, saying, "This is
finally me, for the first time really me."
Yet why not
mix in Latin rhythms?
Our poetry has the provinces in its blood,
and arrives astonished at the world.

Here Lives the Jewish People

The life in the towered city
burns in white fires.
And on the streets of the Jewish East Side
the white fires burn even whiter.

I love to wander in that blaze of the Jewish East Side,
squeeze my way through that crush of stalls and pushcarts,
and breathe in the odors
of that humid, bare life.
In that whiteness
bearded Jews appear,
their arms filled with dresses
that hang to their shoes;
and men or women with sick birds
look with longing, eyes pleading
for a customer, to hand him a lucky card;
and Jews in wheelchairs,
blind cripples who sit, sunk in the shoulders,
who see with their shoulders the color and size
of the coins dropped into a hat –
then a hidden longing wakes in me,
my boyhood longing
to turn into that limping beggar
who used to hobble from street to street in our shtetl
(Luria was his name),
the clack of his crutch on sidewalks, over thresholds.

דאָ וויינט דאָס ייִדישע פֿאָלק

דאָס טורעמדיקע לעבן אין דער טורעמדיקער שטאָט
ברענט אין ווײַסע פֿײַערן.
און אויף די גאַסן פֿון דער ייִדישער איסט־סײַד
ברענט די ווײַסקייט פֿון די פֿײַערן נאָך ווײַסער.

איך האָב ליב אַרומגיין אין דער ברענענדיקייט פֿון דער ייִדישער
איסט־סײַד,
זיך שפּאַרן דורך דער ענגשאַפֿט פֿון געשטעלן און פֿון פּושקאַרטס,
און אָטעמען אין זיך דעם ריח און געזאַלצנקייט
פֿון אַן אָנגעהיצטן נאַקעט־לעבן.
און אַלע מאָל, ווען אין דער ווײַסקייט וואַקסן אויס פֿאַר מײַנע אויגן
ייִדן בערדיקע, אַרומגעהאַנגענע פֿון קאָפּ ביז פֿיס
מיט לאַנגע העמדער מיידלשע און ווײַבערשע;
און ייִדן, אָדער ייִדענעס מיט קראַנקע פֿינגעלעך,
וואָס קוקן מיט פֿאַרבענקטע בעטנדיקע אויגן
אויף אַ קונה צו דערלאַנגען אים אַ מזל־קוויטל;
און ייִדן אויף צוויי־רעדערדיקע שטופּוועגעלעך,
בלינדע קאַליקעס, וואָס זיצן טיף אַרײַנגעזונקען אין די אַקסלען
און זעען מיט די אַקסלען דעם קאָליר און גרײַס
פֿון אַן אַרײַנגעוואָרפֿענער נדבֿה, –
דעמאָלט וועקט זיך אויף אין מיר אַ בענקשאַפֿט אַ באַהאַלטענע,
אַ בענקשאַפֿט נאָך פֿון ייִנגלשדיקע יאָרן,
צו מגולגל ווערן אינעם הינקענדיקן בעטלער,
וואָס פֿלעגט אַרומשפּרינגען פֿון גאַס צו גאַס אין אונדזער שטעטל,
(לוריא איז געווען זײַן נאָמען)
און קלאַפּן מיט זײַן קוליע איבער טראָטואַרן, שוועלן.

Who knows if he
isn't sitting in that very wheelchair
and seeing my amazement through the film coating his eyes.
Then the world wasn't filled with towers,
yet white, like now,
fiery and white, like now.

Hour after hour I walk these streets,
imagining city gates in a fiery whiteness,
and elongated columns
soaring above the dilapidated stalls
toward the white void of New York skies;
and above the portals, signs glowing, flashing,
Here lives the Jewish people.

The life in the towered city
fades into shades of yellow-gray
and on the streets of the Jewish East Side
the yellow-grayness turns more yellow, gray.
Step by step, the men with the long dresses –
for girls, for the ladies – disappear around corners;
and an old woman carries a sick bird,
fortune-telling cards filling the box in the cage.
And here's the blind cripple wheeling home
through the streets cleared of pushcarts and stalls.
Longing stirs in me. I follow
the hard-peaked shoulders of the cripple
(Luria was his name).

װער װײסט, צי זיצט ניט אָפֿט מאָל אױפֿן שטופֿװעגל, װאָס מײנע אױגן זעען,
דער זעלבער בעטלער פֿון מײן ייִנגלשדיקער בענקשאַפֿט,
און זעט דורך בלינדע הײטלעך מײן פֿאַרװוּנדערונג? –
דעמאָלט איז די װעלט געװען נישט טורעמדיק,
אָבער װײס איז זי געװען אַזױ װי איצט,
פֿײערדיק און װײס װי איצט.

איך גײ אום שעההענװײז אין די גאַסן פֿון דער ייִדישער איסט־סײד,
און מאָל אױס פֿאַר מײנע אױגן אין דער פֿײערדיקער װײסקײט
טורעמן פֿאַנטאַסטישע, קאָלאָנען אױסגעשטרעקטע,
װאָס הײבן זיך פֿון איבער אַלע צונױפֿפֿאַלענע געשטעלן
אַרױף צו צו די װײטע אױסגעלײדיקטע ניו־יאָרקער הימלען.
טורעמן, װאָס איבער אַלע זײערע געזימסן
הענגען אָנגעליטע, פֿונקענדיקע שילדן מיט דער אױפֿשריפֿט:
דאָ װוינט דאָס ייִדישע פֿאָלק.

דאָס טורעמדיקע לעבן אין דער טורעמדיקער שטאָט
פֿאַרגײט אין געל־גרױע שאָטנס,
און אױף די גאַסן פֿון דער ייִדישער איסט־סײד
קומט אָן די געלע גרױיקײט געלער־גרױער נאָך;
עס שפֿאַנען טראָט בײ טראָט די ייִדן
מיט די לאַנגע העמדער, מײדלשע און װײבערשע,
און װערן ערגעץ נעלם אױף אַ ראָג;
עס טראָגט די ייִדענע דאָס שטײגל מיטן קראַנקן פֿױגל,
און פֿול איז נאָך דאָס שאַכטל מיט מזלות.
און אָט פֿאָרט אױך אַהיים דאָס בלינדע קאָליקע
דורך גאַסן אָפֿנעלײדיקטע פֿון פֿושקאַרטס און געשטעלן
מײן בענקשאַפֿט װאַקסט אין מיר. איך לאָז זיך גײן
נאָך די האַרטע אױפֿגעשפֿיצטע אַקסלען פֿונעם קאָליקע.
(לוריא איז געװען זײן נאָמען) –

I'm lured by the approach – the entrance to his den,
and then I'm stabbed by the stare of a widening
eye, fixed in the middle of his back.

Quiet. Midnight.
The world has never felt like this before,
so dark, so drenched with night.

And in this darkness the city gates loom,
gates of white flame that looked like a dream during the day
but now reveal their enormous, curved shapes
as thick as the gates of a fortress, gates
encircling, enclosing,
walling in all street corners,
and over the portals red letters warn,
Here sleeps the Jewish people.

Quiet. Midnight.
My boyhood longing cries out in me.

מיך לאָקט דער צונאַנג, דער אַריינגאַנג פֿון זײַן נעסט.

ביז וואַנען, פּלוצלונג, איך דערפֿיל אַ שניידנדיקן קוק אויף זיך,

אַ קוק פֿון אַ צעעפֿנט אויג, וואָס זיצט אין מיטן פּלייצע.

שטיל. האַלבע נאַכט.

אַ מאָל איז די וועלט נישט געווען אַזוי ווי איצט,

אַזוי פֿינצטער און האַלבנאַכטיק ווי איצט.

און אין דער פֿינצטערניש וואַקסן אויס אַן אמת אַן אמת די טיערן,

וואָס זיינען אינעם וויסן פֿלאַם פֿון טאָג געווען נאָר אַ חלום;

זײ אַנטפּלעקן זיך אין זייער גאַנצער גרייס און קײַלעכדיקייט,

רינגלען אַרום און פֿאַרצאַמען און פֿאַרשליסן אַלע ראָגן

ווי דיקע טיערן פֿון פֿעסטונגען.

טיערן, וואָס איבער אַלע זייערע געזימסן

העגנען רויטע און אָרינענדיקע אויפֿשריפֿטן:

דאָ שלאָפֿט דאָס ייִדישע פֿאָלק.

שטיל. האַלבע נאַכט.

עס וויינט אין מיר מײַן בענקשאַפֿט פֿון די יונגלשדיקע יאָרן.

Here Lives the Jewish People

Chemistries of letters buzzing glowing – handwriting
of tubes – enameled goods caught in floodlights –
names and signs visible by day or night – foods yield
Plonsk-odors that penetrate petals on oilcloth
and grain the kitchen's bright linoleum – surprise
mica-glints – sparkles of the pave – grouted borders
touch, bond and isolate each hexagonal tile
in hallways bathrooms vestibules landings –
cracks of dirt insinuate on windowsills
and a pod of women herd on a stoop –
square letters banished to Siberias of newsstands –
circulations impaired by sports horoscopes serried
figures of the Exchange –

    immersion intake inborn –
Yiddish speaking from the navel of a bialy – rye
breads speckled with caraway seeds mistaken for manna –
the bakers' union label pasted to a heel –
goosebumps of plucked chickens tinged blue – flanken
and horseradish – china ringed by the fox hunt –

    quizzical receiver native-alien –
clannish knots and freeform openings smelled and traced
in cigar smoke – tasted in the torques of bow ties – touched
in the gray curls of astrakhan – heard in tongues
gabbling over marble counters – glass casings – registers
    pigeon-breasted –

    the claimed and unclaimed – the felt unknown
in backward Z's in cylinders of locks –

in flutings and notches of keys – in the iceman's
iron forceps clamping the block of ice –
in pie charts of black yomicas – in dark funnels
inwrapped by bolts of fabrics – in the stitch-edged tongues
rising from the instep yet laced into place – geographies
of memories divorced from landscape – Shanghai-
asylum-cousins with cracked Baltic snapshots – suffix-
towns of...ejka...ozyn...odka – in the basement
cubicle leather bleaches under baggage straps
and buckles of pocked mold –

    where borders shift –
then our leaping like a bridge to Manhattan –
to the fawn-stoned Whitney, to the vitreous MoMA –
aligned with "choiring strings" –
our nesting in rooms never carpet-bombed to rubble flanking naked
dusty streets – but we ensconced – like a candle
giving light to the mirror of itself – as we revel in
our flight beyond the East River –

    ignorant claimant heir unapparent –
yet storehouse of sounds – magazine of jokes – repository of retail –
smuggling under customs – trafficking in the modern –
reading in the subway-orphanage of yellow bulbs –
gripping the black cartilage of the chipped enamel straps –
and our vessels bright along the quayage – cordage,
tackle, netting – lifeboats slung from the davits –
the specter-white names of our home ports
high on the edge of the hull

To America

It's been forty-one years now that I've lived between your borders,
    America,
and have carried within me the fruits of your freedom
consecrated and blessed by the sacrificial blood of Lincoln
and the hymns of Walt Whitman. Yet see – how strange, that I'm still
    looking
for an answer to my contradictions, to the unrest of my life,
and I ask myself: why is it that up to now I haven't sung to you
in joy, in praise, in pure admiration,
in accord with your spaciousness, your states, your byways,
your prairies and your mountains and valleys, and, even more,
my four small walls – when I lived in Brownsville, or on Clinton St.,
or in Boro Park, or in the Bronx, or in the Heights;
and most of all: the many times I strolled along East Broadway –
that East Broadway that even now excites me
with tribal intimations the minute I step on its streets.

It's been forty-one years now that I've lived under your skies,
and for more than thirty of them I've been a citizen,
yet, until today I couldn't find in myself either the words
or the means to describe my arrival, my taking root in your land,
to describe the expanding revelation that you are, America.
As soon as I was about to speak to you, I hemmed in my words,
made them rigid, kept them in check,
bound them in tight-fisted knots, my whole world and my whole life
hidden under secret locks, far from your wide latitudes.
Now I must confess something to you: When I disembarked
forty-one years ago and stepped on your earth, I wanted
to fall down and kiss you. Yes, yes – I wanted to, and I should have,
but I didn't do it… Later, on your blessed earth,

צו אמעריקע

שוין איין און פֿערציק יאָר אַז כ׳לעב אין דיינע גרענעצן, אַמעריקע,
אַז כ׳טראָג אין זיך די ברכה פֿון דיין פֿרייהייט, – יענע פֿרייהייט
וואָס איז געהייליקט און געבענטשט געוואָרן דורכן קרבן־בלוט פֿון
לינקאָלן,
און דורך די הימנעס פֿון וואָלט וויטמאַן. זע, ווי אויסטערליש: איך זוך
נאָך היינט אַז ענטפֿער אויף די סתּירות, אויף דער אומרו פֿון מיין לעבן,
און כ׳פֿרעג: פֿאַר וואָס האָב איך ביז היינט נאָך ניט באַזונגען דיך
מיט פֿרייד, מיט לויב, מיט לויטערער באַוואונדערונג,
ווי ס׳פֿאַסט פֿאַר דיינע רחבֿותן, פֿאַר דיינע שטעט, פֿאַר דיינע וועגן,
פֿאַר דיינע פּרעריס און פֿאַר דיינע בערג און טאָלן. און נאָך מער:
פֿאַר מיינע קליינע וועגן – אַ מאָל אין בראָנזוויל, און אַ מאָל אין
קלינטאָן־סטריט,
אַ מאָל אין באַראָ־פּאַרק, אַ מאָל אין בראָנקס און אין די הײַטס,
און מער פֿון אַלץ: פֿאַר אַלע מיינע פֿוסשפּאַצירן איבער איסט בראָדוויי, –
די איסט־בראָדוויי וואָס פֿילט אויך היינט מיך אָן מיט אויפֿגעהײַטערטקייט,
מיט היימישדיקער אייגנקייט, ווי נאָר איך שטעל מיין פֿוס אויף איר אַרויף.

שוין איין און פֿערציק יאָר אַז כ׳לעב אונטער די הימלען דיינע,
שוין העכער דרייסיק יאָר אַז כ׳בין אַ בירגער דיינער,
און – כ׳האָב ביז היינט אין זיך ניט נאָך געפֿונען, ניט דאָס וואָרט
און ניט דעם אופֿן ווי אַזוי מיין אָנקום און מיין אויפֿקום אויף דיין ערד
צו מאָלן ברייט אַנטפּלעקעריש ווי דו ביסט עס אַליין, אַמעריקע.
ווי נאָר עס איז געקומען וועגן דיר צו רייד, האָב איך געצאַמט
די ווערטער מיינע, זיי פֿאַרשטיפֿט אין שטרענגער אײַנגעהאַלטנקייט,
געבונדן זיי אין צימצום־קנופֿן. גאָר מיין וועלט און גאָר מיין לעבן
געהאַלטן אונטער סודותפֿולע שלעסער, ווײַט פֿון דיין צו אָפֿענער
פֿאַרנעמיקייט.

and in memory of my father, I wrote poems of guilt and longing,
and I said to his spirit: "Even as late as it is, accept
my kisses that ever since childhood I wanted to give you, that I should
    have given you;
but I was ashamed to kiss you"… and even in your greatness, America,
surely you won't insist that you are more to me, closer to me, than
    my own father.

And perhaps you will reply: "I am not more, but am I any less
    deserving?"
Actually, I would love to hear you say this,
because to hear it is soothing to my heart,
and I would like to be able, even in the sunset of my days,
to unlock those confessions I've kept from you, America.
I say once again, I've tried to do that through hundreds of hints
in stanza and rhyme, in the pace of tragic dialogue,
in the rising and falling of a curtain. Again and again I've tried
to tear the curtain away from my own heart,
to become open and intimate with you, America, to be even
half as intimate as I am with the little cemetery in Ihumen,
where my father and mother lie amid far-off days,
those far-off days sunk in the deluge of World War One;
to be half as intimate as I am with the glaring snows of my tiny
    village Vittim
in Irkutsk-Yakutsk in the wilds of Siberia;
half as intimate as I am with Isaac's tread to Mt. Moriah, and with
    Mother Rachel's tomb;
with David's prayers and with Isaiah's radiant prophecy,
with Hirsh Lekert's ascent to the gallows after shooting the governor
    of Vilna,
with the dancing through the night at kibbutz Ein-Harod.

איך זאָג אַצינד דיר אויס: ווען כ׳בין אַרונטער פֿון דער שיף

מיט איין און פֿערציק יאָר צוריק, באַרירט דיין ערד, – האָב איך געוואָלט

מיט מיינע ליפן צופֿאַלן צו איר און קושן זי. יאָ, יאָ, געוואָלט, געזאָלט

און – כ׳האָב עס ניט געטאָן . . . אויף דיין געבענטשטער ערד דערנאָך

האָב איך, אין זכר פֿון מיין פֿאָטערשער געשטאַלט, געשריבן שולד־ און

בענקשאַפֿט־לידער,

און כ׳האָב צו דער געשטאַלט געזאָגט: נעם צו אין מיין פֿאַרשפֿעטיקונג

די קושן וואָס איך האָב, נאָך זיענדיק א קינד, געוואָלט־געזאָגט

און אייביק זיך געשעמט צו געבן דיר... אין גאָר דיין גרויסקייט

וועסטו, אַמעריקע, געוויס ניט פֿוילן ביי זיך צו זאָגן

אז דו ביסט מער, אז דו ביסט ייחוסדיקער, בילכער פֿון מיין טאַטן.

און אפֿשר וועסטו זאָגן וועגן זיך: איך בין ניט מער, צי בין איך אָבער

ווייניקער? –

פֿאַר וואָר – כ׳וואָלט זייער וועלן הערן ווי דו זאָגסט עס.

ווייל ווען איך הער עס, וואָלט עס זיין א באלזאַם פֿאַר מיין האַרץ,

און כ׳וואָלט געוואוינט, כאַטש אין דער שקיעה פֿון מיין לעבן, עפֿענען פֿאַר דיר

די אַלע נאָך איינגעשלאָסענע ווידוויים וועגן דיר, אַמעריקע.

כ׳זאָג נאָך א מאָל – איך האָב פרוביערט עס טאָן דורך הונדערטער רמזים

פֿון פֿערז און גראַם, דורך אויפֿברויזן פֿון טראַניק־דיאַלאָגן,

דורך אויפֿגעהויבענע און פֿאַלנדיקע פֿאַרהאַנגען. איך האָב געזוכט

ניט איין מאָל ווי אַזוי אַראָפֿצורייסן פֿון מיין איינן האַרץ דעם פֿאַרהאַנג

צו ווערן אָפֿן און אינטים מיט דיר, אַמעריקע, כאַטש העלפֿט פֿון דעם

ווי כ׳בין אינטים מיט דעם בית־עולמל פֿון קליין איהומען,

וואו ס׳לינן מיינע טאַטע־מאַמע די פֿאַרגאַנגענע אין יענע וויטע טעג,

אין יענע וויטע טעג פֿאַרמבולדיקע פֿון דער ערשטער וועלט־מלחמה;

ווי כ׳בין אינטים מיט די צעגליטע שנייען פֿונעם דערפֿעלע וויטים

אויף די אירקוטסק־יאַקוטישע פֿאַרלוירנקייטן פֿון סיביר;

ווי כ׳בין אינטים מיט יצחקס נאָנג צום באַרג מוריה און מיט מוטער רחלס

קבֿר.

I've tried – and it's clearly *my* fault and not yours
that thirty years ago, under your skies, I grieved deeply,
complained to myself that I carry my Yiddish poems steeped in sorrow
and anxieties through your streets and your squares,
clenching my poems between my teeth the way an alley cat carries
her kittens, looking for some quiet corner in a cellar.
When I think of my brothers – Yiddish poets –
their fate grips me, and I want to say a prayer for them – wishing
them some good fortune – and immediately all my words are struck
    dumb.
Clearly, it's *my* fault, and not yours, that even today,
more than thirty years later, my heart is steeped in a new elegy;
for now, even more than before, an evil fate has flung
all Yiddish poets into new Siberias,
tossed our floundering poetry-ship into a chaos of storms,
a chaos of storms even in your waters, America,
into deadly peril; and in that very peril I seek a bold poem
of a bold captain, a bold captain who even now doesn't betray
    his fateful poem.
You see – I'm too hard on myself when I say: "Clearly, it's my fault,"
when, instead of "clearly," I'd like to say "perhaps" or "probably."
I'm trying hard not to cast any blame on you, America.
And God Himself is a witness that you are still not worthy of feeling
entirely free from guilt, entirely white as snow.
You see – you should have helped me just now to find
the right words, words that can bear nearness and fusion and farewell,
fusion with all of your beauty and all of your breadth.
Farewell? – The greater the fusion, the closer we come to imagining
the moment of parting. It can happen within your borders,
or it can happen far away, beyond your borders:
It can raise me and carry me off to those wondrous landscapes

ה. לייוויק

מיט דודס תפילות און מיט ישעיהס ליכטיקער נבואה,
מיט לעקערטס אויפֿגאַנג אויפֿן תליה־קנופ און מיט די אויפֿגאַנגסטענין פֿון
עין־חרוד. –

איך האָב פרובירט, – און קלאָר איז, אַז ס׳איז מײַן שולד און ניט דײַן
וואָס, נאָך מיט דרײַסיק יאָר צוריק, האָב איך אונטער די הימלען דײַנע
געטרוױערט טיף אין זיך, געקלאַנגט זיך אַז איך טראָג מײַן ייִדיש ליד
אין אַנגסט, דורך דײַנע גאַסן און דורך דײַנע סקווערן,
פֿאַרקלאָמערט צוויושן מײַנע ציין, וי ס׳טראָגט אַ קאַץ אַן עלנטע
די קעצלעך אירע, זוכנדיק פֿאַר זיי אַ רוערט אין אַ קעלער וו; –
אַז וען איך טראַכט נאָר וועגן מײַנע ברידער – ייִדישע פֿאָעטן –
נעמט זייער גורל וי אַ קלאַמער מיך אַרום, און ס׳וילט זיך תפֿילה טאָן
פֿאַר זיי,
פֿאַר זייער מזל, – און גראָד דעמאָלט וערן אַלע וערטער שטום.
אָודאי איז עס מײַן שולד, און ניט דײַן, אויך הײַנט, ווען נאָכן אָפֿגאַנג
פֿון יענע דרײַסיק יאָר טוט טרוױערן מײַן האַרץ אויף ס׳נײַ עלעגיש
וואָס הײַנט, נאָך מער וי וען עס איז, האָט ס׳בייזע מזל
צעשלײַדערטערט אַלע ייִדישע פֿאָעטן איבער ניט־סיבירן,
און אונדזער פֿלאַטערדיקע דיכטערשיף פֿאַריאַנט אין תהום פֿון שטורעמס,
אין תהום פֿון שטורעמס אויך אויף דײַנע וואַסערן, אַמעריקע,
אויף טויט־סכנה; און אין דער טויט־סכנה זוך איך ס׳בראַווע ליד
פֿון בראַוון קאַפֿיטאַן אויך הײַנט. דער בראַווער קאַפֿיטאַן זאָל ניט פֿאַרראַטן
זײַן גורל־ליד אויך הײַנט. – – –
דו זעסט – איך בין אַכזריותדיק צו זיך ווען כ׳זאָג: אָודאי איז עס
מײַן שולד,
ווען כ׳וואָלט געקאָנט אַנשטאָט „אָודאי" זאָגן; אַפֿשר און מסתמא.
איך היט מיך פֿון צו וואַרבן כאַש אַ טייל פֿון שולד אויף דיר, אַמעריקע.
און גאָט אַליין אין הימל איז אַן עדות אַז דו ביסט ניט ראָי נאָך
צו פֿילן זיך אין גאַנצן ריין פֿון שולד, אין גאַנצן וייס וי שניי. – – –

59

where as a child I wandered with Father Abraham
around Beersheba, and with David around the gates of Jerusalem;
even now it can lift me to New Jerusalem.

You too, America, have walked intimately with them,
for you have also taken to heart God's command and blessing
to be a land that flows with milk and honey,
to be as abundant as the sands on the shore and the stars in the sky,
to be a prophet of freedom just as your founders dreamed you could be.
O, let the dream of Walt Whitman and of Lincoln also be your dream.

Now in my old age, when I stand in the clear view
of one or another bright farewell—I remember once again
that moment forty-one years ago when I reached your shore,
America, and I wanted to and I should have
thrown myself down and put my lips to your earth,
but, confused, bewildered, wasn't able to do so—
let me do it now, truly, even as I stand, embraced
by the radiance of coming closer and saying farewell, America.

September 12, 1954

דו זעסט – אין דער מינוט וואלטסטו אליין באדארפֿט צו הילף מיר קומען
און מאכן גרינג מיר דאס געפֿינעניש פֿון יענע ווערטער,
וואס טראגן אי התקרבֿות, אי צונויפֿגיסונג און אי געזעגענונג.

צונויפֿגיסונג מיט אל דיין שיינקייט און מיט אל דיין גרויס צעאטעמטקייט;
געזעגענונג? – וואס גרעסער די צונויפֿגיסונג, אלץ נענטער קאן געמאלט זיין
די רגע פֿון צעזעגענונג. זי קאן געשען אין דיינע גרענעצן,
זי קען אבער געשען אויך וויַיט, מחוץ פֿון דיינע גרענעצן: –
זי קען מיך אויפֿהייבן און מיך אוועקטראגן צו יענע וווּנדערערטער,
ווּ כ׳בין נאך יינגלווייז ארומגעגאנגען מיט אברהם אבֿינו
ארום באר-שבֿע, און מיט דוד ן ארום די טויערן פֿון ירושלים,
זי קאן מיך ברענגען אויך צו היַינטיקע ארויפֿגאנגען פֿון ניַי-ירושלים.

אויך דו, אמעריקע, ביסט נאנט מיט זיי ארומגעגאנגען,
אויך דו האסט אין דיַין הארץ פֿארנומען גאטס געבאט און ברכה
צו זיַין א לאנד וואס רינט מיט מילך און האניק,
צו זיַין פֿילצאליק ווי דער זאמד ביַים ים און ווי די שטערן אויפֿן הימל,
צו זיַין נבֿיאיש פֿריַי, ווי ס׳האבן דיר געחלומט דיינע שעפֿער. –
א זאל דער חלום פֿון וואלט וויטמאן און לינקאלן אויך היַינט דיין חלום זיַין!

אין טעג פֿון עלטער, ווען איך שטיי אין העלן אנגעזיכט
פֿון דער, אדער פֿון יענער ליכטיקער צעזעגענונג, – דערמאן איך ווידער זיך
אן דער מינוט, ווען כ׳האב מיט איין און פֿערציק יאר צוריק
דערגרייכט דיַין ברעג, אמעריקע, און כ׳האב געוואלט און כ׳האב געזאלט
א פֿאל טאן צו דיַין ערד און צופֿאלן צו איר מיט מיַינע ליפֿן,
און – כ׳האב עס אין פֿארלוירענער צעטומלונג ניט געטאן,
דערלויב עס מיר צו טאן אצינדערט, – ווארהאפֿטיק אזוי ווי כ׳שטיי
ארומגענומען נאָ׳ש דער העלקייט פֿון התקרבֿות און געזעגענונג, אמעריקע.

12טער סעפֿטעמבער 1954

61

Particles

There are small strange animals, known to natural history, snakes or worms, I believe, who, when cut into pieces wriggle away contentedly and live in the snippet as in the whole. So the denizens of the New York Ghetto, heaped as thick as the splinters on the table of a glass-blower, had each, like the fine glass particles, his or her individual share of the whole hard glitter of Israel.

— Henry James, *The American Scene*

1

The sundered inheritance quickens the child, released
chemistries of the tribe dispersed in air, seeping
into him, mingling, changing, disseminating – into
the *shpritz*, the pitch, the probe, the books, the books,
and the noodging, the doubting, the spying, the nosing
out, about, around, toward; the mind sniffing the world,
trusting and distrusting the mustering of knowledge,
'til the reach of the searcher and the tic of the skeptic
took – in the street, the cafeteria, the poolhall, the schoolyard,
the seminar, the comedy club, and the novel (that garner of pity), and
the subways (those carrels on wheels); the language pregnant
    over and over
from the incessant *shtup* of know, know, know – words and affixes
and gibing rhythms of the mother tongue assimilating to the
    general speech.

2

Those lower east side cafes you visited – "torture rooms of the
    living idiom" –

were haunts of partisans and Yiddish poets you would never
    meet or know,
writers, like you, anxious about the fate of their language. And by
    my time,
our resultant English, that you thought would never be called English,
grasped what was happening to us, and then *made* what was
    happening to us,
all this turn of speech devised, and burrowed for, and flexed
    by the mind
quizzing itself because we, children of the "torturers," had
    also read you.

3

Then, that old cycle of going around and coming around
appeared when, nearing his death, Alfred Kazin complained:
"What I miss most of all in New York is hearing English."
Was your own fear being repeated by an ex-ghetto denizen
whose need to cross the bridge into "the city" impelled him
    from Brownsville,
though he returned in the greatest Russian memoir in the language?
Is it different this time, English really being pushed to the back seat,
or simply a new version of an old story, similar strains at work,
the strains I can still sense at work inside of me?
For the past, even now, in New York, is born right before my eyes in
    the brownstones of the 19th century,
the facades, the shadings, the cornices I studied
because that's how I thought I might possess this country,
though, long ago, elements of that city had entered my
    speech and desire
and gesture and exertions – like sperm released into a duct fertile
    with uncertainty.

A Memory (I)

Erev Yom Kippur,
when I was ten,
I went to grandmother Reyzl's
to receive her blessing.
A small, thin widow,
a baker with sunken shoulders,
she suddenly said to me,
"Here, my child, is a kosher strap,
like the one on tephillin;
take it and, as the law says,
give me thirty-nine lashes."
Frightened, I stared,
because I knew that lashings
were given in shul and only to a man.
A slight smile appeared on her lips,
and she said, "Don't be surprised, my child,
I've sinned and deserve to be whipped,
I'm steeped in sins.
What do you expect?
Someone at my age, how
could he not be steeped in sin?
So, my child, take the strap
and give me thirty-nine lashes,
and when you've counted out the full amount,
then with a cleansed heart
I'll give you my blessing,

אַ דערמאָנונג

מײַן אַלטע באָבע רייזע אַ בת־שבעים,
אַ קלייניקנע, אַ דאַרינקע אַלמנה,
אַ בעקערין מיט אויסגעפראַצעוועטע פלייצעס,
האָט איין מאָל, אין אַן ערב־יום־כּיפּור,
ווען איך, אַ ייִנגל אַ צעניאָריקס, בין צו איר געקומען
איר ברכה צו פאַרנעמען, מיט אַ מאָל אַזוי געזאָגט:
– אָט לינט, מײַן קינד, אַ כּשרע רצועה, נעם זי
און גיב מיר, ווי דער דין איז, נײַן און דרײַסיק . . .
און ווען איך האָב אַ קוק געטאָן אויף איר
מיט חידוש און מיט פּחד ווײַל איך האָב געוווּסט,
אַז מלקות גיט מען נאָר אין שול און נאָר צו מאַנספּאַרשוינען,
האָט קוים אַ שמייכל זיך באַוויזן אויף איר ליפ
אַזוי צו זאָגן: חידוש זיך ניט, קינד מײַנס,
כ׳בין זינדיק און עס קומט מיר מלקות,
איך בין אײַנגעטונקט, איך זאָג דיר, אין עבירות, –
אַ קלייניקייט – אַ מענטש שוין איבער זיבעציק
ווי זאָל ער ניט זײַן אײַנגעטונקט אין זינד?
איך זאָג דיר – איך בין פֿול מיט זינד אַריבערן קאָפּ,
טאָ נעם זשע, קינד מײַנס, די רצועה
און גיב מיר נײַן און דרײַסיק מלקות,
און אַז דו וועסט מיר אָפּצײלן די פולע צאָל,
ערשט דעמאָלט וועל איך מיט אַ רייִנעם האַרצן
מײַן ברכה געבן דיר – און צו דער ברכה
וועסטו נאָך האָבן פאַרדינט אַ מיצווה. – – –
און איידער וואָס און ווען, איז שוין די באָבע
געלענן אויף די קני אַרויף צו מיט איר פלייצע,

and in addition to my blessing
you will have earned a good deed."
Before I knew it, my grandmother
got down on her knees, hunched up her shoulders,
"Go to it, give me thirty-nine lashes.
I'm asking you."
So I did what she wanted
and lifted the strap with my right hand
and brought it down gently,
barely touching the dress on her back,
her small, bent back.
But my grandmother was annoyed,
"Don't spare me, whip me
the way a sinful Jew should be whipped."
I whipped harder, and my grandmother began counting
with great pleasure, until she counted out
the full thirty-nine lashes.
Picking herself up from the ground,
filled with gratitude,
beaming – "For my health" –
she pressed me to her,
then placed her hands
on my head, her fingers spreading,
until each finger began to drip a warm prayer;
sweet words, pure as olive oil,
covered both of my temples –
and as she went on, tenderly,
like grass newly sprouting, her prayer,
my shaking, and the flutter of my heart,
became calm, and calmer, and calmer.

און נאָך אַ מאָל געזאָגט מיט הייס געבעט:
נעם שמייס מיך נײַן און דרײַסיק שמיץ, איך בעט.
האָב איך געטאָן דער באָבעס רצון –
געהויבן די רצועה מיט מײַן רעכטער האַנט,
אַראָפּגעלאָזט זי אויף דער באָבעס פּלייצע –
אַ קליינע, אויסגעבויגענע און דאַרע פּלייצע –
געשמיסן לײַכט, קוים אָנגערירט דאָס קלייד.
די באָבע אָבער האָט געמורמלט ניט צופֿרידן:
– ניט שאַנעווע, שמײַס ריכטיק, ווי מען שמײַסט אַ ייִדן.
האָב איך דערפֿילט אויך די בקשה פֿון דער באָבען –
געשמיסן שטאַרקער, און די באָבע האָט געצײלט
מיט גרויס הנאה, ביז איך האָב איר אויסגעטיילט
די גאַנצע נײַן און דרײַסיק שמיץ מיט דער רצועה.
אַ שטראַלנדיקע מיט די ווערטער „צו רפֿואה"
האָט זי זיך אויפֿגעהויבן פֿון דער ערד,
און פֿול מיט דאַנקבאַרקייט מיך צוגעדריקט צו זיך,
געטוליעט מיך צו זיך און אויף מײַן קאָפּ
אַרויפֿגעלײגט די ביידע קליינע הענט אירע,
צעשפּרייט די פֿינגער, און פֿון יעדן פֿינגער
האָט תּפֿילהדיקע וואַרעמקייט גענומען טריפֿן,
און ווערטער זיסע, לויטערע ווי בוימל,
און צאַרטע, ווי אָט ערשט אַרויסגעשפּראָצטע גרעזלעך,
אַרומגענומען האָבן מײַנע ביידע שלייפֿן, –
און וואָס אַ רגע איז דער באָבעס תּפֿילה,
און אויך דאָס פֿלאַטערן פֿון מײַנע ברעמען,
און אויך דער אָטעם פֿון מײַן האַרץ
געוואָרן שטילער, שטילער, שטילער.

A Memory (II)

The rod my father used to beat us
leaned between the oven
and the wall, warning – "I might strike
any time, a child better watch out!"

My father wasn't a strong man,
the work of whipping hard for him;
he scarcely counted out ten lashes
before turning pale and cold.

Worn out, he'd sit on the bench,
hold his hand to his heart, grit his teeth,
and complain to the child he just whipped,
"See, you've made me sick, you thief!"

The beaten child stared at him,
unable to grasp the words, not knowing
what he'd done to deserve it,
baffled by the strange complaint.

Meanwhile, my mother ran for water,
pouring out resentment through her tears:
"Why did you hit the child? He was quiet as a rabbit!"
My father couldn't hear a word.

He fainted on the bed,
drops of cold sweat on his white forehead.
See – the whipped child beats his breast.
See – the whipped child revives the flogger.

א דערמאָנונג

אין ווינקל פֿון אויוון האָט געשטעקט די רוט,
מיט וועלכער דער טאַטע האָט די קינדער געשמיסן,
געשטעקט ווי אַ וואָרענונג, אַז יעדע מינוט
קאָן קומען די שטראָף – און אַ קינד זאָל עס וויסן!

דער טאַטע איז קיין גרויסער גיבור ניט געווען,
איז שווער אים אָנגעקומען די מלאָכה שמייסן,
ביז וואַנען ער דערצײַלט די שמיץ קום ביז צען,
נעמט אַ קאַלטע בלאַסקייט אַרום דעם כעסן.

ער בלײַבט אַן אויסגעשעפּטער זיצן אויף דער באַנק,
ער כאַפּט זיך בײַם האַרץ און פֿאַרקלעמט די ציינער,
נעמט טענהן צום געשמיסענעם: מאַכסט דאָך מיך קראַנק,
וואָס האָסטו צו מיר, דו גזלן איינער?!

דאָס קינד דאָס געשמיסענע קוקט אים אָן,
עס קאָן ניט באַגרײַפֿן די ווערטער זײַנע;
קיין שמיץ ניט פֿאַרדינט, ווייל קיין שלעכטס ניט געטאָן –
דאָס קינד בלײַבט געפּלעפֿט פֿון דער מאָדנער טענה.

די מאַמע דערווײַל לויפֿט נאָך וואָסער אַ גלאָז,
דערבײַ לאָדט זי אויס איר פֿאָרדראָס דורך טרערן:
– וואָס האָסטו צום קינד? ס׳איז דאָך שטיל ווי אַ האָז!
איר וואָרט אָבער קאָן שוין דער טאַטע ניט הערן.

דער טאַטע פֿאַלט צו אין חלשות צום בעט,
מיט שווײַסאָנגסטן טראָפֿנט זײַן שטערן זײַן ווײַסער,
און זע – דער געשמיסענער שלאָגט זיך על־חטא,
און זע – דער געשמיסענער מינטערט דעם שמײַסער.

Father Legend

The old Jewish cemetery of Ihumen
in thick wild grass, abandoned.
I have not come to this old cemetery
to curse or to lament,
but to receive a blessing
from under a mound.
Autumn. Moss on the mound,
sun on the moss.
All of my limbs –
the strings of an instrument –
and moving over the strings – a hand
of someone who rises from death
and comes back to life:
"Son, you are here.
Good. Good.
Your smile – let it rise
not over these graves, but gardens.
My blood pours out in this sunshine –
overflows into another body.
Who is this other body –
Tree – the tree in the forest is this other body,
threshold – the threshold of our home on Berezene St.
is this other body.
Oh, my boy, my boy –
It is I, your father,
I with the red beard.
Let your hands carry every touch of mine,
let your lips carry my kisses,
kisses I wanted to give you,
that I should have given you,

ה. לייוויק

טאַטע־לעגענדע

דער אַלטער בית־עולם פֿון איהומען
אין ווילדקייט פֿאַרוואַקסן, פֿאַרלאָזן.
און איך בין צום אַלטן בית־עולם געקומען
ניט פֿאַר געפֿלוך און געיאָמער,
נאָר ברכה פֿאַרנעמען
פֿון אונטערן בערגל.
האַרבסטיקער מאָך – אויפֿן בערגל,
זוניקער טאָג – אויפֿן מאָך.
אין מיר אַלע גלידער – ווי סטרונעס,
און איבער די סטרונעס – אַ האַנט
פֿון איינעם, וואָס שטייט אויף פֿון טויט
צו ווידערגעבוירט:
– זון, דו ביסט דאָ.
גוט. גוט.
זאָל אויפֿניין דײַן שמייכל
ניט איבער קבֿרים – נאָר בײַטן.
אין זוניקייט גיסט זיך אַריבער מײַן בלוט –
גיסט זיך אַריבער אין אַ גוף פֿון אַ צווייטן.
ווער איז דער צווייטער?
בוים, וואָס אין וואַלד, איז דער צווייטער,
שוועל פֿון דער שטוב אויף בערעזענער גאַס –
שוועל איז דער צווייטער.
ייִנגל דו מײַנער, ייִנגל דו מײַנער,
איך בין דײַן טאַטע דער רויטער.
טראָג אויף דײַן האַנט מײַנע אַלע באַרירן,
טראָג אויף דײַן מויל מײַנע קושן,
וואָס איך האָב געוואַלט און געזאָלט
און אייביק געשעמט זיך דיר געבן.

71

but always shame held me back,
and also my words,
which in my poverty and in my sadness
stammered – –
Lying under the earth
I have seen light from your life,
light from your heart,
opening to me only after death.
Lying under the earth
I have heard all of your cries,
seen all of the pain and suffering
of each new daybreak
in your remote and lowered eyes.
Lift your eyes and see
how much light is over you,
over our poor home
where you gave your first cry
in white, legendary Kislev.
Lying under the earth,
light opened up to me,
truth revealed itself to me –
that on the day you will come
(and I knew that you would, that you must!)
I will receive you
with clear,
good,
lucent words."

So spoke my father
from the grave.

ה. לייוויק

און אויך מײַנע ווערטער,
וואָס איך האָב אין אָרעמקייט,
וואָס איך האָב אין טרויער
פֿאַרשטאַמלט – – –
ליבנדיק אונטער דער ערד,
געזען האָב איך ליכט פֿון דײַן לעבן –
ליכט פֿון אַ האַרץ,
וואָס ערשט נאָכן טויט ווערט עס אָפֿן.
ליבנדיק אונטער דער ערד
געהערט האָב איך אַלע געשרייען,
געזען אַלע פֿײַנען און שטראָפֿן
אין אויפֿגאַנג פֿון נײַטאָג
אין דײַנע אַרונטערגעלאָזטע דערוויטערטע אויגן.
הייב אויף דײַנע אויגן
און זע, וויפֿל ליכט איבער דיר,
און איבער דעם שטיבל
ווּ דו האָסט געגעבן דײַן ערשטן געשריי
אין ווײַסן לעגנדישן קיסלוו.
ליבנדיק אונטער דער ערד
האָט ליכט זיך צעעפֿנט,
האָט וואָר זיך אַנטפֿלעקט – איך זאָל קענען
אינעם טאָג, ווען דו'רסט קומען,
(און קומען, געווּסט האָב איך, מוזסטו!)
דיך אויפֿנעמען
מיט קלאָרע,
מיט גוטע,
מיט ליכטיקע ווערטער. – – –

אַזוי האָט געֿרעדט מײַן טאַטע
פֿון אונטערן קבֿר.

73

Leivick

I want to dance naked,
gaze at Bathsheba. I want
to live in the mountains
and valleys of Cezanne's tablecloths,
near oranges, a ginger pot, a vase,
dresser drawers with oval-plated
keyholes and concave knobs.
I want to stand before his tables,
altars of fruit.

I peeled my tongue from the iron
bar, drew it back into my mouth,
a childhood prank turned to winter's blood.
The Czar's police smashed in my door,
caught me red-handed, seized
my pamphlets and printing press,
threw me into solitary.
I huddled with my hallucinations.
Four years later I slogged through the snows,
ended up here on Essex, pasting epaulettes
for nightclub doormen, drum majors,
and generalissimos under movie marquees.

Even in New York the Cossacks
whip their horses through my poems.

A Small Sheet of Paper

Of the thousands of things in my world, the only ones remaining from
    childhood
are a small sheet of paper, completely blank, and an old pen –
and what would happen if something were written on that sheet of
    paper?
To ask such a question will only make people laugh out loud.

And if that happens, am I afraid of such laughter?
No, only I'd suddenly be at odds with myself:
"If you're a true poet, the genuine article –
set down, as beautifully as you can, your very last poems on that sheet
    of paper."

Day and night I put off doing just that, day in and day out I put it off,
writing on other, on all sort of papers,
making sure I overlook that old sheet of paper, wanting to forget it,
forcing my fingers to not even touch it.

I myself don't know what to make of my evasion.
Is it dread – of some soul being re-embodied in me?
And more than that I don't know – and what will happen to me
if I turn into someone else when that sheet gets written on.

א ביינעלע פּאפּיר

פֿון טויזנט זאַכן אויף דער וועלט איז מיר פֿון קינדהייט נאָך פֿאַרבליבן
אַ ניט פֿאַרשריבן ביינעלע פּאפּיר און אויך אַן אַלטע פֿעדער –
איז וואָס וועט זיין, ווען ס׳ביינעלע וועט ווערן שוין פֿאַרשריבן?
פֿון פֿרעגן נאָר אַזוינס קאָן הויך אַ לאַך טאָן יעדער, יעדער.

און אַז ער וועט אַ לאַך טאָן? האָב איך מורא פֿאַר געלעכטער?
אָ ניין, נאָר איך אַליין מיט זיך אַליין ווער פֿלוצלינג קידער–ווידער:
„אויב דו ביסט יאָ אַ דיכטערמאַן אַן אמתער, אַן עכטער –
פֿאַרשרייב דאָס ביינעלע מיט שיינקייטן פֿון סאַמע לעצטע לידער."

איך צי אָפּ טעג און נעכט, איך צי אָפּ הונדערטער מעת–לעתן,
איך שרייב אויף אַנדערע, אויף נײַע אַלערלייַיקע פּאפּירן,
נאָר ס׳אַלטע ביינעלע פֿאַרזע איך, ווי צו וועלן עס פֿאַרגעסן,
כ׳מייד אויס, אַז מײַנע פֿינגער זאָלן עס אפֿילו ווען באַרירן.

איך ווייס אַליין ניט, וואָס מיין אויסמיידן באַדאַרף באַטײַטן.
צי האָט זיך ניט אין מיר אַזאַ מין גילגול–שרעק פֿאַרקליבן?
און מער נאָך ווייס איך ניט, צי כ׳דאַרף זיך אויף אַן אנדערן פֿאַרבײַטן,
און וואָס וועט זיין מיט מיר, ווען ס׳ביינעלע וועט זיין פֿאַרשריבן.

77

Uri Zvi Greenberg

(1894 - 1981)

Recognition

And not just those, who speak as I speak
and pray to the same God of the patriarchs
when stars come out or light glows in the east,
are my only brothers –

But also those, who, in quivering moments,
when stars rise and dark orphanhood
falls from all worlds on the beaten paths,
wander quietly, lonesome as shadows,
and long for four walls and a ceiling,
heads bent,
lips murmuring…

And not just those who wrap themselves in prayer shawls
for *Shakhres*, when golden light pours outside,
and bells ring from the church belfries,
and the pious Jews cannot unite with the divine in their thoughts
because the clanging of the bells unhinges their concentration –

Shakhres – Jewish morning prayers

אורי־צבי גרינבערג

(1981 - 1894)

באַקענונג

און נישט נאָר די, וואָס רעדן גלײַך ווי איך רעד
און בעטן צו דעם זעלבן גאָט פֿון ד׳אָבֿות
בײַם שײַן פֿון שטערננעכט און גאָלד פֿון מיזרח,
זענען מײַנע ברידער ד׳אײנציקע -

נאָר די, וואָס אין די צאַפֿלדיקע רגעס,
ווען שטערן גייען אויף און אויף די שליאַכן
פֿאַלט טונקל יתומקייט פֿון אַלע וועלטן,
שטיל וואָגלען זיי, די אײנזאַמע, ווי שאָטנס,
און בענקען נאָך פֿיר ווענט און נאָך אַ באַלקן,
קעפּ געבויגן,
לעפֿצן מורמלענדיקע . . .

און נישט נאָר די, וואָס הילן זיך אין טלית
שחרית-צייט, ווען דרויסן גיסט דאָס גאָלד זיך,
און גלאָקן קלינגען פֿון דעם הויכן קלויסטער,
און ס׳קענען נישט די פֿרומע האַרץ ייחוד
מיט דעם אלהות אין די מחשבֿות,
ווײַל יעדער גלאָקנקלאַנג איז זיי מבֿלבל -

But also those, who fall, covered in dust,
somewhere amid fields of white crosses,
and who want to pour themselves out, like waves of water –
their hands wringing,
mouths in the grass…

And not just those, whose virgin bodies
no eyes see, except their mothers' eyes
and the white walls of their parents' dwelling,
are my only sisters –
but also those, whose wanton bodies
are like trees on the windblown Steppes,
and who stroll streets in the blazing noon sun,
and as late as midnight, though it's raining,
and have no tears for their misfortune…

And not just those, who cut their hair
on those gray mornings after weddings,
in the restfulness of sweet homes, God, faith,
and can unite with their husbands, who have immersed themselves
        in the *mikve* –
but also those who, during November nights filled with sadness,
in the blinding ocean-lights of electric lamps,
in the raucous buzz of foreign soldier-voices,
drink beer after beer and let the drunkards
wildly have their way…

נאָר די, וואָס פֿאַלן, שטויב באַדעקט, וווּ ערגעץ
אין מיטן פֿעלדער בײַ די ווײַסע צלמים,
און ווילן זיך צעגיסן ווי אין כוואַליעס –
העגט צונויפֿגעבראָכן,
מויל אין גראָזן . . .

און נישט נאָר די, וואָס זיי׳רע מיידל־גופֿים
זעט קיין אויג נישט, חוץ דער מאַמעס אויגן
און ווײַסע ווענט אין טאַטע־מאַמעס־ווינען,
זענען מײַנע שוועסטער ד׳איינציקע –
נאָר די, וואָס זיי׳רע גופֿים זענען הפֿקר,
ווי די סטעפּעסבײַמער אין די ווינטן,
און שפּאַנען דורך די גאַסן אין דעם זונבראַנד
ביז אין שפּעטע חצותן, כאַטש עס רעגנט,
און האָבן נישט קיין טרער פֿאַר זייער אומגליק.

און נישט נאָר די, וואָס שערן זיך די האָר אָפּ
אין יענע גראָע מאָרגנס נאָך די חופּות,
אין רו פֿון זיסע היימען, גאָט, בטחון,
און קענען זיך באַהעפֿטן צו די מאַנצביל,
וואָס האָבן זיך געטובֿלט אין דער מיקווה –
נאָר די, וואָס אין נאָוועמבער־נעכט פֿול טרויער,
אין גרעלן ים־ליכט פֿון עלעקטער־לאָמפּן,
אין הייסן זשום פֿון פֿרעמדע זעלנער־קולות,
טרינקען ביר אויף ביר און לאָזן טועןן
די שיכורים זיי׳רע ווילדע ווילנס – –

And not just people with deep souls,
who have eyes, hearts, and lips,
into whose intimacy I can pour out my heart,
are my only friends –
but also abandoned dogs, who scamper,
looking for little bones under butcher blocks,
and from a distance I squeak to one of them:
"Psst, psst." He comes and climbs up my knees
and we look in each other's eyes...

And not even just dogs,
who yowl under fences in the moonlight,
when my heart can't contain itself and pours
into an ocean of chants and prayer-tears,
are my only friends –
but also God's beings that are silent:
wild oaks in remote forests;
gray cliffs,
ready to be embraced...

און נישט נאָר מענטשן מיט נשמות טיפֿע,
וואָס האָבן אויגן, הערצער, הענט און ליפֿן
אין וועמענס נאָנטקייט כ׳קען מײַן האַרץ צעגיסן,
זענען מײַנע פֿרײַנד, די אײנציקע,
נאָר די פֿאַרלאָזטע הינט, וואָס לויפֿן זוכן
אונטער יאַטקעקלעצער פֿיצלעך קנאָכנס,
און כ׳רוף מיר איינעם מיט אַ פֿיפֿס פֿון ווײַטנס:
קום! ער קומט און שטײַנט אויף מײַנע קניעס
און איינס דעם צווייטן קוקן מיר אין ד׳אויגן – –

און נישט נאָר הינט אַפֿילו, הינט, וואָס קלאָגן
אין לבֿנה־נעכט פֿון אונטער פּלויטן,
ווען מײַן האַרץ ווערט פֿול צום איבערגיסן
אין געזאַנגען־ים און תּפֿילה־טרערן,
זענען מײַנע פֿרײַנד, די אײנציקע,
נאָר גאָטס באַשעפֿענישן אויך, וואָס שווײַגן:
ווילדע דעמבעס אין אַ פֿרעמדלאַנד־וואַלדונג,
גראָע פֿעלדזן צום אַרומנעם גרייטע – –

[I drink marrow and blood]

I drink marrow and blood from the full springs of my women —
they call me the holy vampire of their period —
then, when the rest-days of my surfeit come,
I bolt my doors, not wanting to see them anymore.

And then my women cry deep into the night,
their long hair falling out, their hair that covered me.
Writhing bodies at the doorstep of my dwelling,
they plead each night, plead each night for pity.

But Venus hovers over my roof,
and a woman in my room waits for me to touch her,
and the teeming lust unfolds and plays between us…
stars, nightfall… the air spiced with sin.

Someone in me says: "Coax the woman: *You are my world*";
and my lips tremble: "You are my whole world!"
The deceived woman opens her veins —
I gnaw and gnaw at that essence and the woman says nothing.

אורי־צבֿי גרינבערג

[איך טרינק מאַרך און בלוט]

איך טרינק פֿון מײַנע פֿרױענס פֿולע קװאַלן מאַרך און בלוט,
זײ רופֿן מיך דער הײליקער װאַמפֿיר פֿון זײער צײַט,
און ס׳קומען דאַן די אָפֿרוטעג פֿון מײן באַזעטיקונג –
שליס איך מײַנע טירן אָפֿ, איך װיל זײ מער נישט זען.

און ס׳װײַנען דאַן די פֿרױען מײַנע אין די טיפֿע נעכט.
עס פֿאַלן אױס די לאַנגע האָר, װאָס האָבן מיך פֿאַרדעקט.
און ס׳קאַרטשען זיך די גופֿים אױף דער שװעל פֿון מײַן געמאַך
און בעטן, בעטן רחמים נאָך, אין יעדן אױפֿדערנאַכט.

אָבער ס׳שטײַט דער װענוס־שטערן איבער מײַן געבײַ,
און אין מײַן שטוב איז דאָ אַ פֿרױ, װאָס װאַרט אױף מײַן באַריר;
און ס׳זיצט די שװאַנגערדיקע תאװה צװישן אונדז און שפֿילט . . .
די שטערננאַכט פֿאַלט צו, די לופֿט מיט בשמימדיקע זינד – –

זאָגט עמעצער אין מיר: רעד אײַן דער פֿרױ: דו ביסט מײַן װעלט,
און ס׳ציטערן די ליפֿן מײַנע: ביסט מײַן גאַנצע װעלט!
– און ס׳עפֿנט אירע אָדערן די אָפֿגענאַרטע פֿרױ –
איך נאָג און נאָג דאָס תמצית אױס און גאָרנישט זאָגט די פֿרױ.

85

[In broad daylight]

In broad daylight, I sense myself in the night
and that sleep that draws me into a sleep in the night.
How can that be? – Perhaps it's a harbinger-tug
toward that sleep in the earth's bed: eternal night;
above it all, winter blizzard, dew and rain, flowering trees.
I see my street and dwelling as if I'm in the after-life,
changed, no longer here in body,
and in broad daylight – night-blue, stars –
I see my house: "none went out, and none came in."

When night falls on light blonde hair
and the head turns night-dark gold,
I would like of course, my dearest,
to bring you to my mother's home
to spend the night on the bed made by my mother's good hands:
the night is full with the scent of apple and forest –
For God's sake! Who's listening? Oh, my God!
Your gold and your body are beautiful in poems!
But in my awakening pain everything's incinerated again –
mother into smoke, you too – not even in a pit –
Jesus-crosses hammered into my mother's home.

[אין מיטן העלן טאָג]

אין מיטן העלן טאָג דערפיל איך אויפֿדערנאַכטיקס
ס׳ציט ציען שלאָפֿן מיך אַ שלאָף אויפֿדערנאַכטיקס.
שוין זשע? – אפֿשר איז עס אַ הקדמה־צייונג
צו יענעם שלאָף אויף ערד־געלעגער: אייביק נאַכטונג.
און איבער אַלעם שנייזאווי, טל־וּמטר, בײַמער־בלײונג.
איך זע מײַן גאַס און ווינונג ווי פֿון יענער וועלט שוין
כאַטש איך בין דאָ בגילגול־גוף גלײַך שוין נישטאָ
אין מיטן העלן טאָג אַ שטערננאַכט איז בלאָ
איך זע מײַן הויז: אין יוצא ואין בֿאָ.

אַז אַן אויפֿדערנאַכט פֿאַלט צו אויף די העל בלאָנדע האָר
ווערט דער קאָפ פֿאַרנאַכטיק טונקל גאָלד,
וואַלט איך מײַן טײַערע אוודאי דיך געוואָלט
ברענגען אין מײַן מאַמעס שטוב
נעכטיקן אויפֿן געבעטן געלעגער פֿון מײַן מאַמעס גוטע העענט.
די נאַכט איז מלא־ריח פֿון עפל און פֿון וואַלד . . .
ווי ווי, צו וועמען רעד איך? ווי געוואַלד!
ס׳איז שיין אזוי אין ליד דײַן גאָלד און דײַן געשטאַלט!
אָבער אין בהקיץ־ווי איז אַלעס אָפֿגעברענט
די מאַמע מיטן רויך, דו אויך, אפֿילו נישט אין גרוב –
אויפֿגעקלאַפֿטע צלמים־ייזלעך אין מײַן מאַמעס שטוב.

Perets Markish

(1895 - 1952)

[Slivers]

Now that my vision's needled inward, my eyes
rip open and each one of my nerves sees
my heart has fallen, like a mirror on a stone,
and with a clang it shatters into pieces.

Is it possible that each one of the splinters
will testify against me to the end of my days?
Don't press me – you Old Ideals – don't judge me
till I've recovered every sliver from the breakage.

I try to join them together, piece
by piece. My fingertips sparkle and bleed. Yet
no matter how artfully I match the pieces
I only see myself cracked and jagged.

In the midst of my despair I near a solution, a
black shape – oblique, lean – looms out of my grief.
I see my own shadow behind the mirror, whose silver
pieces are scattered over the field of my life.

פּרץ מאַרקיש

(1952 - 1895)

[בראָכשטיקער]

אַצינד, װען ס׳קערט די ראיה מיר זיך אום צוריק אַלײן,
איז מיר אַ ריס די אױגן עפֿענען און זען מיט יעדן גליד דאָ,
אַז ס׳איז מײַן האַרץ אַראָפּגעפֿאַלן, װי אַ שפּיגל אױף אַ שטײן,
און מיט אַ קלונג אַ קלאַנג פֿון בראָך אױף שטיקער זיך צעשפּליטערט.

געװיס איז אױך אײדערער בראָכשטיק ניט באַפֿרײַט
צו זײַן אַז עדות װען מיר ביז מײַנע לעצטע פֿיר באַשערטע אײַלן.
- צעטרעט מיך נאָר ניט, דו, - אָ, ריכטער מײַנער, צײַט,
ביז איך װעל אָפּזוכן אין אױסזאַמלט די צעשפּריצטע טײַלן. . .

איך װעל זײ אױפֿקלײַבן פֿאַרפֿרװוּן - אײנס צו אײנס -
באַהעפֿטן זײ בײַנאַנד, ביז בלוט אין פֿינגער זיך פֿאַרשטאָכן, -
- כאָטש װי איך זאָל זײ קונציק ניט צונױפֿקלעפּן, אַלץ אײנס
װעל איך אין דעם זיך שטענדיק זען פֿאַרקריפּלט און צעבראָכן.

ערשט איצטער קומט צו מיר אין טרױער דער באַשײד,
אין װי פֿון איבערשמעלץ - באַגרײַף איך פֿלאַמיק
דעם פֿײַן פֿון װעלן זען זיך אין שפּיגל - גאַנצערהײט,
װאָס איז אין בראָכשטיקער צעזײט אױף אַלע שבֿעה ימים. . .

[Sadness grows in hands]

Sadness grows in hands, like gold in autumn,
and a clear, clear evening nests in the eyes:
My destined lover, death! For you I gather my beginnings
      and my endings,
just as a poor blind man gathers a groschen to a groschen.

Deep in the gorge of myself, a source beseeches me,
the way brimming buckets slosh up from a deep well,
and I wait here, as if at a harbor or a terminal,
the train overdue, still on the other side of twilight.

For so long, I neither fasted nor prayed.
Thirsts whip out from my body, like flames from a blaze,
and consume my days like sleepy villages.

Oh, poor bookish body, pent up in your thirsts –
sought by a slaughtering knife sharpened ceaselessly on endings –
like a bull – from a dark slaughter house – you've escaped...

1923

פּרץ מאַרקיש

[אומעט וואַקסט אויף העענט]

אומעט וואַקסט אויף העענט, ווי גאָלד אויף אָסיען,
און צו די אויגן טוליעט זיך אַ העלער, העלער אָוונט:
– באַשערטער מײַנער, טויט! פֿאַר דיר נאָר קלײַב איך מײַנע אָנהייבן
און סופֿן,
ווי ס׳קלײַבט אַ בלינדער אָרעמאַן אַ גראָשן צו אַ גראָשן!

צוריק אין זיך אַליין זיך בעטן הייזעריקע קוואַלן,
ווי ס׳רײַסן זיך צוריק אין טיף פֿון ברונעם – פֿולע עמער,
איך וואַרט דאָ נאָר אַזוי אויף האָפֿענס און וואָקזאַלן,
פֿאַרשפּעטיקט האָט די באַן, וואָס פֿירט אויף יענע זײַטן דעמער.

כ׳האָב אַזוי לאַנג שוין ניט געפֿאַסט און ניט געדאַוונט,
עס שלאָגן דאַרשטן פֿונעם לײַב, ווי פֿון אַ שׂריפֿה – פֿלעמער,
און מיטן פֿײַער טראָגן זיי אַוועק די טעג, ווי דערפֿער שלאָפֿנדע.

– אָ, אָרעם בחור־לײַב, געפֿענטעוועט אין דאַרשטן־קלעמער, –
אַ חלף זוכט דיך אום, געשלײַפֿט אָן סוף פֿון אַלע סופֿן,
ווי אַ בוהײַ – פֿון שלאַכטהויז פֿינצטערן – אַנטלאָפֿענעם!.. .

1923

Reading Markish

"My destined lover, death!
(Basherter mayner, toyt!)"
my friend bristles.
"Not simply everybody's destiny,
but to be in love with death!
When I was in the camps
I wanted to live, not die."

   "I am half in love with easeful death"

"It's a Yom Kippur poem
(S'iz a yomkiper-lid)"
I tell my friend –
"fasted prayed whip.
Within death, fear, loss,
and longings that tear him apart,
psalmist Markish seeks his life."

   "Lisp'd to me the low and delicious word death"

"I prefer writers who face death
(Ikh hob beser lib shraybers vos kukn dem toyt in ponem arayn)
like Bashevis and Tolstoy,
who do not play around with it,
weaving theories about life.
I have seen too much of it. Markish
isn't serious. He's infatuated with his words."

"Death is the mother of beauty; hence from her,
Alone, shall come fulfillment to our dreams
And our desires"

"We're talking about different things
(*Mir redn veygn farsheydene zakhn*).
That destined loss can spur us to life,"
I explain, tractable in my abstractions.
Then, still sensing the body of my friend's voice,
I add, "Sometimes I think my ideas only come
from my mind, or what I've read."

"Deep in the gorge of myself, a source beseeches me"

As I leave, my friend and I embrace.

Moyshe Kulbak

(1896 - 1940)

I have seen...

I have seen Yiddish words like licks of flame,
like sparks rising from dark ore.
I have felt Yiddish words like birds without a home.
My heart longs for the birds
fluttering in air.

משה קולבאַק

(1940 - 1896)

געזען האָב איך...

געזען האָב איך ייִדישע ווערטער ווי פֿייערלעך קליינע, ווי
פֿייערלעך קליינע,
ווי פֿונקען געצוינען פֿון פֿינצטערן אַרץ.
געפֿילט האָב איך ייִדישע ווערטער ווי טײבעלעך ריינע, ווי
טײבעלעך ריינע.
די טײבעלעך וואָרקען און וואָרקען אין האַרץ...

95

Yiddish

O Yiddish,
I felt your teeth
in my bones.
You cut into my childhood body
like the saw of a bungling magician
that bit through
the woman in the coffin.
Now I comb the stage
of the abandoned theater
for every splinter,
every chip I can lay my hands on.
Where are the bloodstains
that show the clumsy act was here?

It's good to know
you're good for nothing now,
except for the love I show you.
We could never have come together
if you were still teeming on the streets,
re-inventing yourself for textbooks,
commercials, psychotherapy.

You reach for me like a lover
wanting one more kiss.
How long it's taken for us to embrace,
for our tongues to find each other.

RICHARD J. FEIN

Reading Yiddish

Far from sheer flourish – like Arabic
or Hindi – your meaning
hinges on dents and hooks –
sense still welded to frame –
my eyes like fingertips on Braille –
couriers of shapes to the brain –
and in reading you I span the years
back to a charactery of childhood – words
on butcher shop windows countering
the flow of English – transliteration
on the dry goods sign – your sounds estranged
in the very characters which conveyed them –
trapping me at family councils – your fecund rasp
perplexing – useless – European – But now
my need to kiss you and change
you into a princess – or at last –
the veil lifted – to see the beauty
you always were – to love that jaw
I once feared to touch – to feel
my fingers graze your throat – And now
I see your shapes always lurked
within – claiming and re-claiming – sounding
my old distress and disavowal –
all that bewilderment
become a source – and out of abasement
emerges your lush runic intelligence –
my native intelligence – as if
I write in a boustrophedon of Yiddish
and English – the Yiddish line unseen –
like the secret-agent letters I wrote
in invisible ink during childhood

97

Reproof, Reply, Desire
(for Marcia Karp)

Yiddish: You have been snug in me, in the sounds
and mouths of me, but you have not sensed
me in my here and now
(mir in mayn itstikayt),
my daily generation in being alive
(mayn tog-teglekhe shafung fun lebm).
I can be heard in the sandbox, over
the counter, across the table.
I'm still alive and kicking
(Ikn bin nit arop fun mark).
I am not only what you need me to be.

Poet: Yiddish Vilna gone, Yiddish Warsaw too.
Klez festivals – with your old rouged face.
I caress you; you murmur; my arms
hold the loving specter of you.

Yiddish: Your argument is not convincing. You limit me.
But I belong to others, who know
me in ways you do not. Yet, I concede
what you have done has also quickened me.

I wish your love of me had gone a bit further.
Halevay volt dayn libe far mir gegangen a bisl vayter.

Jacob Glatstein

(1896 - 1971)

Great World of Quiet Wonder

Not worn-out, played-out, but
wonder on my shining roof.
A bird dreams of droplets of rain in his throat,
of seeds strewn from a sill.
I am mirrored in a bead of water.
The world contracts
to the dimensions of my room.

A country-stillness surrounds me.
Flowers bloom, breathe, in the very withering.
A man carrying a bucket of milk
just now drawn from a cow
startles me with his "Good morning,"
as if he plays on the udder of a bagpipe.
A downcast woman plucks the prison bars of a harp.
A child's hands toy with one another in a crib.
Clucking, quacking, fluttering –
a yard of chickens, hens, geese.
A girl with sad eyes
shadows herself in the sun with a green hat.
She sings for herself, and her song
comes back toward her along the way.

יעקבֿ גלאַטשטיין

(1971 - 1896)

גרויסע וועלט פֿון שטילן וווּנדער

נישט אויסגעפֿייניקט – אויסגעטענוגט האָב איך דיך,
וווּנדער אויף מײַן צעשפּיגלטן דאַך.
אַ פֿויגל פֿאַרחלומט אַ שלוק רעגנבלײַב אין זײַן ליבן האַלדז.
איך שפּיגל זיך אין מינדסטן טראָפּן
און זע די גרויסקייט וואָס האָט זיך פֿאַר קליין פֿאַרשטעלט.
אין די דלד אמות פֿון מײַן בענקען,
שפּרייזט די רחבֿות פֿון גאָר דער וועלט.
אַרויס דורך טיר און פֿענצטער,
זינגט דאָס פּעטיטע וווּנדער פֿון מײַן געצעלט.

אַרום מיר אַ פֿאַרפֿוערטע שטילקייט.
עס אָטעמט בלום אין בלי און ס׳לעבט בלום אין וועלק.
אַ מאַן טראָגט אַ שעפֿל מיט שוימיקן געמעלק
און כאַפּט מיך אויפֿן שאַרף פֿון זײַן גוט־מאָרגן.
אַ פֿאַרוואָלקנטע פֿרוי צופֿט די סטרונעס פֿון אן אײַטערדיקער
האַרף.
אַ קינד שפּילט זיך מיט די הענטלעך אין אַ וויגל.
געגודער פֿון געפֿלינל.
געזעגנג און געטענץ פֿון העגער און הינער,
קאַטשקעס און גענדז.
ס׳איז גרויסער טאָג.
אַ פֿלאַטער איז אָנגעפֿלויגן און אַוועק.
אַ מיידל מיט טרויעריקע אויגן

101

In a world of such light
an unexpected night has fallen.
An echo responds:
"Dark crowns sing on the trees.
Roofs sparkle against the night,
and all small, daily wages
turn into cries, into laughter.
My unexpected planets wheel
above your riven deaths."

The lips of the girl sing again.
I fear her Lorelei voice. Yet I see
a fleecy moon at midday,
a scattered sun at night.
I speak to the great world of quiet wonder,
di groyse velt fun shtiln vunder:
"Put me to sleep for a thousand years,
yet I will still remember
how the shadows of wires
parcel light in the snow,
and year in and year out
I will long
for the tiny wonder of my room."

שירעמט זיך קעגן זון מיט אַ גרינעם הוט.
זי זינגט פֿאַר זיך און אויף די וועגן קומט אַנטקעגן איר געזאַנג:
צו דער וועלט פֿון אַזוי פֿיל ליכטער,
איז געקומען אַ פֿאַרנאכט אַן אומגעריכטער
און פֿאַרשיידערט מיט שטילשווײַג און דערוואַרטן.

און אַ נאָקול ענטפֿערט אָפּ:
די נאַכט פֿינצטערט איבער שטילע ברויטן.
אייביק איז מײַן וועלט פֿון ליכט.
איבער אַלע דײַנע משוגענע טויטן
גייט אויף מײַן שטערן אומגעריכט.

דאָס מיידל מיט דעם גרינעם הוט האָט פֿאַרשאַטנט איר אייגן געזאַנג:
די גרויסע וועלט פֿון שטילן וווּנדער,
פֿלעמלט אין פֿאַרנאַכטיק ליכט.
און אין יעדן פֿאַרדרימלטן אויג באַזונדער,
שטערנט אויף אַ חלום אומגעריכט.

דאָס נאָקול ענטפֿערט אָפּ:
אויף די בײַמער זינגען טונקעלע קרוינען.
די דעכער שפֿיגלען זיך אַנטקעגן נאַכט,
און אַלע קליינע, בײַטאָניקע לוינען,
ווערן איצטער ווײַנענדיק פֿאַרלאַכט.

דעם אָוונטיקן דועט טראַכט איך אָן אַזוי אויף זיך:
ווי ווייניק וועלט ס'איז מיר באַשערט,
ווערט דאָס וווּנדער נישט פֿאַרקליינט.
און האָב איך עפּעס באַזונדערט און צעשטערט,
ווערט עס איצטער צוריקגעבויט און פֿאַראיינט.

An evening duet plays in my mind:
How little of the world was destined to be mine,
how little of the world I knew how to enter,
and yet its wonder has never diminished.
What I have missed or ruined
returns, saying, "Brood, yet live with us."

דאָס מײדל זינגט מיט רוזֿנדיקע ליפֿן.
דאָס לאָרעלײ־קול שלעפֿערט און שרעקט.

מײנע אויגן ווערן זעעוודיקער און גרעסער,
מײנע אויגן ווערן אויפֿגעפֿלעקט.
דאָס מײדל פֿאַרשווינדט, דאָס נאָכקול פֿאַרטונקלט.
די נאַכטיקײט ווערט אָפּגעהילט פֿון טאָג.
און צו דער באַפֿעלעריששער שטילקײט
גיב איך אַזוי אַ זאָג:
גאָט פֿון אַל די רוען,
פֿאַראײצטיק מיך אויף שטענדיק,
מיט מײן חלום און מיט מײן וואָר.
דעם לעצטן ניגון לעש אויס, פֿאַרענדיק,
און פֿאַרגליווער מיך אויף טויזנט יאָר.
און טויטערהײט וועל איך געדענקען
דעם אָוונטשײן אויף אַ ליכטיקער וועלט,
און יאָר־אײן יאָר־אויס שטאַרקער בענקען,
נאָך דעם פּעטיטן וווּנדער פֿון מײן געצעלט.

Maybe You

What is the source?
The room? The tent? The world?
Maybe just you.
You, you, always you,
everywhere you.

I saw you rise yesterday,
like a small hand on a blazing patch of sky,
and I have come to comprehend you,
because you were smaller than me.
The hand was the hand of a wife,
the hand of a caress,
the hand on a quiet, small bed.

I have fallen on my face.
I have come to comprehend you.
I have prayed words
which were sweet to your palate.
I have come to comprehend you.

אפֿשר דו

וואָס איז דער מקור?
די שטוב? דאָס געצעלט? די וועלט?
אפֿשר גאָר דו.
דו, דו, אַלע מאָל דו,
אומעטום דו.

כ׳האָב דיך נעכטן געזען אויפֿגנײן
ווי אַ קלײנע האַנט אויף אַ צעפֿלאָמט שטיקל הימל.
און כ׳האָב דיך באַנומען,
ווײל ביסט געווען נאָך קלענער פֿון מיר.
די האַנט איז געווען אַ האַנט פֿון אַ ווײב,
די האַנט פֿון אַ גלעט,
די האַנט אויף אַ שטיל, קלײן בעט.

כ׳בין געפֿאַלן אויפֿן פּנים.
כ׳האָב דיך באַנומען.
כ׳האָב געדאַוונט ווערטער
וואָס זײנען געווען זיס צו דײן גומען.
כ׳האָב דיך באַנומען.

What is the source?
Understanding.
You have risen like a single
shining letter in me.
I have read you
with every touch.
I take off clothes.
Girl-like earth,
on which I travel –
so much devotion,
so much abundance –
is holy.

What is the source?
You are holy, not just some times,
but each and every separate time – holy.
Because you have always burned,
like a thornbush,
but never burned up in your fire.
A sad, intelligent God,
between me and you,
is like a lamp that is turned down,
growing darker and darker.
He is not angry,
does not think of punishment;
He is a divine shadow
over our restless sleep.

וואָס איז דער מקור?
פֿאַרשטייִקייט.
ביסט אויפֿגעגאַנגען ווי אַן אייניציקער
ליכטיקער אות אין מיר,
כ׳האָב דיך געלייענט
מיט יעדער באַריר.
כ׳צי אַרונטער די שיך,
כ׳צי אַרונטער די קליידער.
די מיידלשע ערד וואָס אויף איר איך טרעט,
מיט אַזוי פֿיל געטריישאַפֿט,
מיט אַזוי פֿיל זעט,
איז הייליק.

וואָס איז דער מקור?
ביסט הייליק, אויב נישט דרײַ מאָל,
ביסטו יעדער באַזונדער מאָל הייליק.
ווײַל דו האָסט אַלע מאָל געברענט
פֿאַר מיר ווי אַ דאָרן
און ביסט שיר נישט אַליין פֿאַרברענט געוואָרן.
אַ טרויעריקער, פֿאַרשטענדיקער גאָט,
צווישן מיר און דיר,
ווי אַ לעמפל, וואָס דרײט זיך אַרײַן,
טינקעלער און טינקעלער.
ער בייזערט זיך נישט
און טראַכט נישט פֿון שטראָף,
נאָר איז אַ געטלעכער שאָטן
איבער אונדזער אומרויִקן שלאָף.

109

A Sunday Over New York

Only churches can be as calm,
as houses are now, glowing with calmness.
The houses have no belfries
but the windows sing quietly.
Only church choirs
can sing so calmly
to a swooning God
who even forgives his torturers.

As if thousands of white roses
had opened their little lips,
the stones of the houses bloom and smell now
in the autumn chill.
Brick walls and steel
are breathed in deeply,
like the powerful and delightful arboreal origin
of a forested city.

Sunday kindles in New York
a joy of childish faith.
Each and every block
turns into a garden, a village,
with blue borders
moist like dew.
The many-storied houses
are rid of the angry ups-and-downs.
They rest like shaped wonders,
as if God had created not only the world
but these as well –
these giant candles with golden wicks,
clement shadows already resting upon them.

אַ זונטיק איבער ניו־יאָרק

בלויז קלויסטערס קענען זײַן אַזוי רויִק,
ווי ס׳זײַנען איצט ליכטיק מיט רו די הײַזער.
די הײַזער האָבן נישט קיין גלעקער
אָבער די פֿענצטער זינגען שטיל.
בלויז קלויסטערכאָרן
קענען זינגען אַזוי רויִק
צו אַ פֿאַרחלשטן גאָט
וואָס האָט אַפֿילו פֿאַרגעבן זײַנע פֿײַניקער.

ווי טויזנטער ווײַסע רויזן
וואָלטן געעפֿנט די פֿיסקלעך,
אַזוי בליִען און שמעקן איצט די שטיינער פֿון די הײַזער
אין דעם האַרבסטיקן פֿרעסטל.
מען אָטעמט טיף אַרײַן
מויער און שטאָל,
ווי אַ קרעפֿטיקע און מחיהדיקע ווימשטאַמיקייט
פֿון אַ פֿאַרוואַלדיקטער שטאָט.

ס׳זונטיקט איבער ניו־יאָרק אַ פֿרייד
פֿון אַ קינדיש גלויבן.
יעדער באַזונדערער בלאָק
ווערט פֿאַרגאָרטנט, פֿאַרדאָרפֿישט
און אַרומגעזוימט מיט בלוי
וואָס איז טויִק.
פֿון די הויכצענאַרנטע הײַזער האָט זיך אָפּגעטאָן
זייער געבויטער און בײַזער צעקלעטער.
זיי רוען ווי געשאָפֿענע וווּנדערס,
ווי גאָט וואָלט באַשאַפֿן
ניט נאָר די וועלט,

How assured churches are
(never seized
by the terror of pogroms),
their old walls
so planted and rooted.

The air is savory
with the aroma of the city-earth,
which smells now like autumn wine
from the rich rot of grape.
And everything that during the week
reeked of iron, gasoline and money
smells now like grass
that the blade of the autumn chill
has just cut.

I go around among the good-natured peasants of the city
and quell all my cries in me.
My big-city synagogue
clamors to me from far away,
but I withdraw into the Sunday-Pale.

נאָר אױך זײ –
די ריזיקע לעכט מיט די גילדענע קנױטן,
שױן מיט די שאָטנס חסד װאָס רוען אױף זײ.

װי זיכער ס׳זיַנען קלױסטערס,
(װיַל ס׳איז זײ קײן מאָל נישט באַפֿאַלן
קײן איבערשרעק פֿון פֿאָנראַמען,)
אַזױ פֿאַרפֿלאַנצט און פֿאַרװאָרצלט
שטײַען די אַלטע מױערן.

די לופֿט אין באַטעמט מיט דעם אַראָמאַט
פֿון דער שטאָטישער ערד,
װאָס שמעקט איצט װי האַרבסטיקער װײַן
פֿון אַ צונעפֿױלטער טרױב.
און אַלץ װאָס האָט אין דער װאָכן
נעעיפֿושט מיט אַלט־איַזן, געזאַלין און געלט,
שמעקט איצט װי גראָז,
װאָס די שאַרף פֿון האַרבסטיקן פֿרעסטל
האָט נאָר װאָס אָנגעשניטן.

כ׳גײ אַרום צװישן די גוטמוטיקע פּױערים פֿון דער שטאָט
און שטיל אײַן אין זיך
אַלע מיַנע געשרײַען.
ס׳ליַערעמט צו מיר פֿון װיַטן
מיַן גרױסשטאָטישע שול,
אָבער כ׳גײ אָפֿ פֿון איר עטלעכע תחום־זונטיק.

113

I'm quiet, like a distant guest,
while gentle eyes and sun-razored faces
smile at me.
I carry toward them a quiet Sunday,
like a bouquet.
Someone speaks to me,
and my own speech sounds
like trembling bells.
The Christian city rests,
and all my old calamities sleep restlessly.
I return to my lonely synagogue.
It stands now also steeped in Sunday-dread.

Tomorrow our wounds
will cry out again,
but the voices of the city
will outshout them again.

כ׳שוועבֿ מיט דער פֿאַרלעגנקייט פֿון אַ גאַסט,
אַז עס שמייכלען צו מיר
צערטלעכע אויגן און זונראַזיירטע פּנימער.
כ׳טראָג זיי אַנטקעגן אַ שטילן זונטיק
ווי אַ בוקעט.
מע רעדט צו מיר
און מײַנע אייגענע ריײד קלינגען
ווי צ׳טערדיקע גלעקלעך.
די קריסטלעכע שטאָט רוט
און מײַנע אַלע אומגליקן דרימלען אומגעדולדיק.
כ׳קום צוריק צו מײַן איינזאַמער שול.
זי שטייט איצט אויך אײַנגעזונטיקט אין שרעק.

מאָרגן וועלן אונדזערע ווונדן
ווידער נוואַלדעווען,
אָבער די קולות פֿון דער שטאָט
וועלן זיי אַריבערשרײַען.

Yankev Glatshteyn Visits
Me in the Coffee Shop

I was facing the back
and didn't see him come in.
He shimmied into the booth
and I knew him right away.
He looked at me, clamped his lips. Sighed.
"I deliberately speak to you
in English because I want you
to understand me perfectly.
Since I died, by the way,
my English is better. I have
long conversations with Marianne Moore
about prose in poetry
and I exchange tales with Yeats –
he's not the snob he used to be.
He tells me a Celtic tale and I
tell him one about Chelm.
It's more literary the life there, but
we don't write anymore.
But that's not what I want to talk about.
It's all good and well you translate me.
You need it more than I do.
I'm in Yiddish for all time.
Not that I mind, mind you.
Be my guest. But you,
you have to translate yourself
into English. Stop fretting
about starting late. Be like Yiddish
literature – grow into your gift.

Don't brood over your unmetrical ear.
Listening to the truth-rattles in you,
your ear will catch on. By the way,
I never mourn Yiddish anymore.
We gather in Peretz's salon-cloud –
our Yiddish will last forever there –
though no one blows in from a shtetl,
manuscript in hand.
Well, *zay gezunt*."
Absentmindedly, he eased away the sugar pourer,
from where it braced the laminated menu,
and his fingers played in the glass fluting;
as he moved out
he jarred the table
and my coffee shook.

B. Alkvit-Blum

(1896 - 1963)

Your Grass

I think of your grass, Whitman,
and hear the stir of the great
stone forest Manhattan.

ב. אלקוויט־בלום

(1896 - 1963)

דיינע גראָזן

כ׳טראַכט פֿון דיינע גראָזן, וויטמאַן,
און הער דעם רויש פֿון גרויסן
שטיינערנעם וואַלד מאַנהעטן.

119

Chrystie Street

December 1960,
I parked on Delancey,
scuffed into Chrystie's no-man's land.
Berlin-Noguchi playground after hours –
ditches, sand pits,
king-of-the-mountain gravel,
toy rubble,
fun-house cement collars
big enough to garage a Beetle,
honeycombs of terracotta pipes,
anarchist-bomb firepots,
a yellow steam shovel's
dipper claws perched by the trench.

Storefront quarters.
Downstairs, Catholic-Worker wards
where the homeless bedded;
upstairs – Ginsberg cawing *Kaddish*,
hip to hip fur and dungarees.
Our Russian poet jamming
the loft-stadium.

Izi Kharik

(1898 - 1937)

August

August. I have come to a shtetl.
August – a cool evening, transparent
and blue; a sad smile rises in smoke
and at dawn the shtetl rises in dew.

Nimble air in the summer mist,
with warmth and light from far away,
air with a heady smell of apples,
and my heart also lush and full…

Not long ago I cursed and condemned you,
now, dear shtetl, you lie gravely still…
I wander in a haze of blossoms and fruits,
and August lies here, transparent, cool.

August, 1925

איזי כאַריק

(1937 - 1898)

אַווגוסט

אַווגוסט. איך בין אין שטעטעלע געקומען.
איז אַווגוסט קיל, און דורכזיכטיק, און בלוי,
צו אָוונט רייכערט זיך אַ שמייכלענדיקער אומעט
און פֿאַר טאָג גייט אויף דאָס שטעטעלע אין טוי.

ס'איז לופֿטיק-גרינג אין זומערדיקן נעפּל,
פֿון הייכן ווײַט מיט וואַרעמקייט און ליכט,
סע שמעקט די לופֿט מיט ווײַניק-קלאָרע עפּל
און אין האַרצן ווערט אויך ווײַניק און געדיכט. . .

איך האָב ניט לאַנג געשאָלטן און געפֿלוכט דיך,
לינסטו איצטער, שטעטעלע, פֿאַרשטילט. . .
גיי איך אַרום אין רויך פֿון צוויט און פֿרוכטן,
און אַווגוסט ליגט דאָ דורכזיכטיק און קיל.

אויגוסט 1925

For Three Killed by Stalin

I think of Bergelson groveling, pleading at the trial, then shot
  by a firing squad on his sixty-eighth birthday;
of Mandelstam freezing, psychotic, with "paralysis of the heart"
  in the gulag;
of Babel spilling his guts about spying, terrorism, parasitism
  in the interrogation chambers of Lubyanka.
I think of them far from their novels, poems and stories, far
  from their faces on the covers of their books;
holding onto another prisoner, who feeds them, helps them walk,
  listens. But maybe none of this happened and they were alone.
I don't want to read about Mirele walking to the outskirts of a
  shtetl; about foreign embassies and gulls shining along
  the Neva; I don't want to read about a boy and the docks
  of Odessa.
I think of Bergelson, Mandelstam and Babel reduced
  to madness, fear and hunger, curled up and mumbling to
  themselves in their bunks.

Then I read them again, forgetting how they died.

Aaron Zeitlin

(1899 - 1974)

Text

All of us –
stones, people, shards of glass in the sun,
jars of jam, cats and trees –
are illustrations of a text.

Somewhere, no one needs us.
There, only the text is read –
pictures fall away like withered leaves.

When death-wind blows in the tall grass
and all the pictures formed by clouds
in the west are swept away –
night arrives and reads the stars.

אַהרן צייטלין

(1974 - 1899)

טעקסט

מיר אַלע —
שטיינער, מענטשן, שערבלעך גלאָז אין זון,
קאָנסערוון־פּושקעס, קעץ און ביימער —
זענען אילוסטראַציעס צו אַ טעקסט.

ערגעץ וווּ דאַרף מען אונדז נישט האָבן.
דאָרט לייענט מען דעם טעקסט אַליין —
די בילדער פֿאַלן וי פֿאַרוועלקטע בלעטער.

ווען טויטווינט גיט אַ בלאָז אין טיפֿן גראָז
און רוימט אַראָפּ פֿון מערב אַלע בילדער,
וואָס וואָלקנס האָבן אויפֿגעשטעלט —
קומט נאַכט און לייענט שטערן.

Children, Always Dying

Children vanish.
Adults – specters
of dead children.

Children, always dying –
even the ones still playing
in the schoolyard, on the stoop,
back of the store, behind the sofa,
in the corner of the bedroom.
Their games are brief –
in a flash they've over.
Adults warn them,
"Don't get dirty."
"Hurry up, we're going."

Children – inventors. Tricksters.
Here one minute, gone the next.

Children vanish.

אַהרן צייטלין

קינדער שטאַרבן שטענדיק

קינדער זענען פֿאַרשווינדער.
גרויסע זענען גילגולים
פֿון געשטאָרבענע קינדער.

קינדער שטאַרבן שטענדיק –
אויך די, וואָס בלײַבן לעבן.
די שפּיל איז קורץ און בלענדיק.
באַפֿעל איז צו זיי געגעבן:
„שנעלער, שנעלער, ענדיק!"

קינדער זענען דערפֿינדער:
זיי האָבן אונדז דערפֿונדן.

קינדער זענען פֿאַרקינדער:
אָננעזאָגט און פֿאַרשוווּנדן.

קינדער זענען – פֿאַרשווינדער.

Six Lines

I know I'm not needed in the world,
me, word-beggar in the Jewish graveyard.
Who needs a poem – and in Yiddish no less?

Only what's hopeless in the world is lovely,
the divine, only what must pass away, and
only submission is rebellious.

אהרן צייטלין

זעקס שורות

כ׳ווייס: קיינער דאַרף מיך נישט אויף אַט דעם עולם,
מיך, ווערטער־בעטלער אויף דעם ייִדישן בית־עולם.
ווער דאַרף אַ ליד – און נאָך דערצו אויף ייִדיש?

נאָר בלויז דאָס האָפֿ־נונגסלאָזע אויף דער ערד איז שיין,
און געטלעך איז נאָר דאָס, וואָס מוז פֿאַרגיין,
און נאָר הכנעה איז מרידיש.

131

All versions of the moon...

All versions of the moon are hidden by the war's smoke
and in that darkness dogs gnaw the marrow from bones,
and gristle that once articulated flesh
and imparted the flex of life
sucked out now to chalky and pocked dumbbells.

All policies foreign,
I am bare
bones in this rubble-annex
century of my own.

Who touches this poem touches a man
wanting the wisdom Tseytlin knew.

Who touches this poem touches a despondent Jew.

August, 2006

Itzik Manger

(1901 - 1969)

Hagar's Last Night in Abraham's House

The housemaid Hagar sits in the kitchen,
a smoky lamp shadows
the shapes of cats and mice
against the gray walls.

She cries. The master ordered
her out of the house today,
"Witch, are you getting out
of my life or not?"

Sarah, matron of the charity box,
kept egging him on:
"Either you get rid of that girl,
or I'm getting a divorce."

Hagar opens her trunk,
pulling out a string of blood-red
beads, a little apron,
silky green, and a straw summer hat.

איציק מאַנגער

(1969 - 1901)

הגרס לעצטע נאַכט ביי אַבֿרהמען

די שיפֿחה הגר זיצט אין קיך,
אַ רויכיק לעמפּל ברענט
און שאָטנט סאַמע קעץ און מײַז
אויף אַלע גרויע ווענט.

זי וויינט. סע האָט דער באַלעבאָס
איר הײַנט געהייסן גיין.
„קליפֿה, האָט ער איר געזאָגט,
דו טרעטסט מיך אָפּ, צי ניין?"

סורטשע די פּושקע־גבאיטע
האָט אים שוין ווידער אָנגערעדט:
„אָדער דו טרײַבסט די דינסט אַרויס,
אַז נישט וויל איך אַ גט."

און הגר נעמט פֿון קופֿערט אַרויס
אַ בײַטשל קרעלן ווי בלוט,
אַ פֿאַרטעכל פֿון גרינעם זײַד
און אַ שטרויענעם זומערהוט.

135

He gave her these things
when they used to take walks
through the meadow, near
where the railroad runs.

"Like smoke from a chimney,
or like smoke from a train –
so, dear mama, so
is the love of a man.

What am I going to do now,
me and his little bastard?
Unless I take him in my hands
and look for housework somewhere."

She takes the broom in her hands
and cleans the room for the last time
and feels something under her blouse
telling her she still loves him.

She does the dishes once more,
and scours the copper pan – –
like smoke from a chimney
is the love of a man.

די זאַכן האָט ער איר געשענקט,
אַ מאָל ווען זיי זענען געגאַן
שפּאַצירן איבער דער לאָנקע,
דאָרט, וווּ עס גייט די באַן.

„אוי, אַזוי ווי אַ רויך פֿון אַ קוימען
און אַזוי ווי אַ רויך פֿון אַ באַן,
אַזוי איז, מאַמע געטרײַע,
די ליבע פֿון אַ מאַן.

וווּ וועל איך מיך איצט אַהינטון
מיטן פּיצל קינד אויף די הענט?
סײַדן נעמען זײַן בענקאַרט
און גיין דינען אין דער פֿרעמד.“

זי נעמט אין דער האַנט דעם בעזעם
און קערט צום לעצטן מאָל די שטוב
און עפּעס אונטער דער בלוזקע
פֿילט, אַז ס׳האָט אים נאָך ליב.

זי וואַשט נאָך אײן מאָל די טעלער
און שײַערט די קופּערנע פֿאַן —
אַזוי ווי אַ רויך פֿון אַ קוימען
איז די ליבע פֿון אַ מאַן.

Abraham Takes Isaac to the Sacrifice

The gray morning-twilight
dawns upon the earth;
old, loyal Eliezer hitches
the black horse to the cart.

Abraham holds in his arms
the son of his old age;
a star, blue and devout,
flashes over the old house.

"Let's get going, Eliezer!" The whip
cracks. The road turns silvery.
(Sad and lovely, says the poet,
are the ways of *Toyreh*.)

Along the road, the gray
willows run backward, hurrying
to see if Sarah's crying
over the empty crib.

"Daddy, where are we going?"
"We're going to the Lashkev fair."
"Daddy, will you buy me something
when we get to the Lashkev fair?"

אַבֿרהם אָבֿינו פֿאָרט מיט יצחקן צו דער עקדה

די גראָע מאָרגן־דעמערונג
דעמערט איבער דער ערד,
דער אַלטער געטרײַער אליעזר שפֿאַנט
אײַן װאָגן די קאָרע פֿערד.

אַבֿרהם טראָגט אויף זײַנע הענט
זײַן בן־זקונים אַרויס
אַ פֿרומער בלאָער שטערן בליצט
איבער דעם אַלטן הויז.

„הײַדאַ אליעזר!" – דאָס בײַטשל קנאַלט
און אָט זילבערט זיך דער שליאַך.
(טרויעריק און שיין, זאָגט דער פֿאָעט,
זענען די װעגן פֿון תנ״ך.)

די גראָע װערבעס פֿאַזע װעג
אַנטלויפֿן אויף צוריק,
אַ קוק טון, צי די מאַמע װיינט
איבער דער פֿוסטער װיג.

„װוּ פֿאָרן מיר איצטער, טאַטעשי?"
„קיין לאַשקעװו אויפֿן יריד."
„װאָס װעסטו מיר קויפֿן, טאַטעשי,
אין לאַשקעװו אויפֿן יריד?"

139

"A soldier made of porcelain,
a drum and trumpet,
and for mother, satin
to cut and sew into a dress."

Abraham's eyes turn moist.
He feels the knife burning
his skin under his gabardine.
"This'll be some fair…"

"Eliezer, see that mill?
You wait over there!
From here on Itzik and I
go on foot."

On the driver's seat, Eliezer
grumbles and stares down the path.
(Sad and lovely, says the poet,
are the ways of *Toyreh*.)

„אַ זעלנערל פֿון פֿאָרצעליי,
אַ פֿייקל און אַ טרומייט
און פֿאַר דער מאַמען אין דער היים
אַטלעס אויף אַ קלייד."

אַבֿרהמס אויגן ווערן פֿײַכט,
ער פֿילט ווי דאָס מעסער בריט
אונטער דער זשופיצע דאָס לײַב:
– שוין איין מאָל אַ יריד. . .

„אליעזר, בײַ דער וואַסערמיל
דאָרט זאָלסטו בלײַבן שטיין!
פֿון דאָרט וועל איך מיט יצחקלען
צו פֿוס שוין ווײַטער גיין."

אליעזר אויף דער קעלניע ברומט
און קוקט אַלץ אויפֿן שליאַך.
(טרויעריק און שיין, זאָגט דער פּאָעט,
זענען די וועגן פֿון תנ״ך.)

141

The Sacrifice of Itzik

Rock me, rock me, blind fate,
I dream with my eyes open, I see –
a great silver bird flying
in from the ocean.

What is that silver bird bringing me?
God knows. Maybe the Kiddush cup
Grandfather held while blessing sweet wine
from the land of Israel?

But who brought up Grandfather's name?
Here he is, coming towards me, the wagon
driver from Stopchet: "Itzik,
the sacrifice is ready."

His eyes burn at me – two stars
shining in the autumn night, his beard
mussed up by the wind and stained
by seven large tears.

Grandfather leads me by the hand toward
cities, villages and ditches – the cities
so small, the villages so large,
and we stride across them.

Grandfather says, "Itzik, do you
remember – a long time ago – an angel
spread his wings above us
and you were saved?

עקדת־איציק

וויג מיך, וויג מיך, בלינדער גורל,
איך חלום מיט אָפֿענע אויגן,
און זע – אַ גרויסער זילבערנער פֿויגל
קומט איבערן ים געפֿלויגן.

וואָס טראָגט פֿאַר מיר דער זילבערנער פֿויגל,
אײן גאָט אין הימל קען וויסן,
אפֿשר מײן זיידנס קידוש־בעכער
מיט ארץ־ישראל־ווײַן זיסן?

נאָר ווער האָט דערמאָנט מײַן זיידנס נאָמען?
אָט שפֿאַנט צו מיר דער זיידע,
דער בעל־עגלה פֿון סטאָפּטשעט:
„איציק, ס׳איז גרייט די עקידה.‟

און זײַנע אויגן ברענען אויף מיר,
ווי צוויי האַרבסטיקע שטערן,
זײן גראָע באָרד איז פֿאַרלאָפֿן מיט ווינט
און מיט זיבן גרויסע טרערן.

פֿירט מיך דער זיידע בײַ דער האַנט
איבער שטעט און דערפֿער און גריבער –
די שטעט זענען קליין, די דערפֿער גרויס
און מיר שפֿרײַזן איבער זיי אַריבער.

זאָגט דער זיידע: „איציק, געדענקסט –
צוריק מיט אַזוי פֿיל יאָרן –
ווען ס׳האָט זיך דער מלאך צו אונדז אַנטפֿלעקט
און דו ביסט ניצול געוואָרן?‟

143

He regrets that, our old God,
and now demands His sacrifice,
though I've lived and I've died
so many times.

Enough's enough. I don't need His mercy.
He shouldn't get the idea, up there…
Good thing your mother's dead, Itzik.
She's spared more tears."

Grandfather leads me by the hand toward
cities, villages and ditches – the cities
so small, the villages so large,
and we stride across them.

איצט האָט ער חרטה, דער אַלטער גאָט
און ער מאָנט בײַ מיר דעם קרבן,
כאָטש כ׳האָב שוין אַזוי פֿיל מאָל געלעבט
און בין שוין אַזוי פֿיל מאָל געשטאָרבן.

אַ סוף, אַן עק, איך דאַרף נישט זײַן גנאָד
און זאָל ער אין הימל נישט מיינען –
איציק, ס׳איז גוט וואָס דײַן מאַמע איז טויט
און זי וועט פֿאַרשפּאָרן צו וויינען."

פֿירט מיך דער זיידע בײַ דער האַנט
איבער שטעט און דערפֿער און גריבער –
די שטעט זענען קליין, די דערפֿער גרויס
און מיר שפּרײַזן איבער זיי אַריבער.

Every Morning
(after a Gypsy song)

Every morning
at the first
sign of light
I ask myself: Where is he?
And I wash my face –
not with clear water,
not with dew,
but with tears
that burn my eyes.

אַיעדן אינדערפֿרי

ציגײַנעריש

אַיעדן אינדערפֿרי
בײַם ערשטן שײַן פֿון ליכט
פֿרעג איך: וווּ איז ער? –
און וואָש מיר דאָס געזיכט,
נישט מיט קלאָרן וואַסער
און נישט מיט פֿײַכטן טוי,
נאָר מיט מײַן הייסער טרער.

Itshe Slutski

(1912 - 1944)

My Father in Brooklyn...

Like pages of a book with a frayed, gray cover,
his 63 years lie open before me:
each line is full with pent-up sadness,
with that silence instilled into a whole generation.

Each word of his speaks of a desolate week,
of painful days and nights – each and every letter:
from 12 years old on he's been carrying around this burden,
this heavy load he drags around with him, never
                    asking, "Why?" –
                    never, "Why?" –

And from Lakhva-Mikashevitsh and from Minsk to as far away
        as Harbin,
the pain drags after him, like a dark-dumb shadow:
he's wandered like a bird without a nest, from land to land,
without a destination, from city to city...

Now I write him a poem, a poem from seven thousand versts away,
by the storm of a sea that swells and subsides:
I stand on its shores and want to pick up a soft whisper,
a whisper from his pages that read themselves...

1936, Danzig

148

איטשע סלוצקי

(1944 - 1912)

מײַן טאַטן אין ברוקלין...

ווי בלעטער פֿון אַ בוך אַ אין טאָוולען אויסגעריבן גרויע
זענען אויפֿגעמישט פֿאַר מיר זײַנע 63 יאָר;
און עס איז אידע שורה פֿול מיט איינגעהאַלטענעם טרויער
און מיט איינגעזאַפֿטן שווײַגן פֿון אַ גאַנצן דור.

נאָר ס׳רעדט פֿון יעדן וואָרט זײַנעם - אַ צערפֿולע וואָך
און אַ פֿײַנלעכער מעת־לעת - פֿון אײדן, יעדן אות;
אַז זינט זײַן 12טן יאָר נאָך, געגאַנגען איז ער שוין אין יאָך,
דעם שווערן עול געשלעפּט אויף זיך און קיין מאָל נישט געפֿרעגט
„פֿאַר וואָס?" - - -
קיין מאָל „פֿאַר וואָס?" - -

און פֿון לאָכוע־מיקאָשעוויטש און פֿון מינסק ביז העט קאַרבין,
דער פֿײַן געשלעפּט האָט געשלעפּט זיך נאָך אים, ווי אַ טונקל־שטומער שאָטן;
געוואַנדערט האָט ער ווי אַ פֿויגל אָן אַ נעסט אָן אַ ווידין,
פֿון לאַנד צו לאַנד און פֿון שטאָט צו שטאָט. . .

איצט שרײַב איך אים אַ ליד, אַ ליד פֿון זיבן טויזנט ווערסט,
מיט שטורעם פֿון אַ ים מיט אויפֿגיין און פֿאַרגיין;
איך שטיי בײַ זײַנע ברעגן און כ׳וויל אויפֿכאַפּן אַ שאָרך
אַ שאָרך פֿון זײַנע בלעטער, וואָס לייענען זיך אַליין - - -

דאַנציק - 1936.

149

Visiting My Father's Grave

I dig,
set down my spade
and cradle in the juniper bush.

> *The worms crawl in,*
> *the worms crawl out,*
> *through the kishkes,*
> *and out the mouth.*

But how could they come out of you?
You, under the lid,
snug in the box.
You, sealed from the dirt,
kept from the grass.

I never threw myself upon your breast.
I never clung to you so you couldn't unloose me.
I never held you firm till you answered me something.
I never touched your lips as I touch those I love.
You never breathed to me the secret of your murmurings.

If you came back
and I were child
we'd still be apart.

What we lacked we lacked together.

The Bay

The bay drowns at night,
drowns and sinks,
gargling water in its wide mouth –
with a dark shudder.

Yet it seems to me
that it sings…
sinks and sings in the night,
marries the night, the
whole night,
till light appears.
And it seems that it laughs
at the whole wide world.

When day comes, day embracing all –
a man is found on the shore: dead.
An empty bottle winks from under his neck.
And from his plugged-up little mouth
words are dragged out (like little black snakes),
words about need, deportation, about dread –
And, "This is why I die."
And, lastly, a request: for "A Jewish burial."

The bay was drunk with the night,
a man – with the bay.
Both, at daybreak, vomited up by the bay.

די בוכטע

די בוכטע טרינקט זיך אין דער נאַכט,
טרינקט זיך און פֿאַרזינקט
און ס׳נאַרגלט זיך דאָס וואַסער אין איר ברייטן מויל –
מיט אַ פֿינצטערדיקן גרויל.

נאָר מיר דאַכט,
אַז זי זינגט. . .
זינגט און זינגט אין דער נאַכט
און איז זיך מתחתן מיט דער נאַכט,
אויף אַ גאַנצענער נאַכט,
ביז סאַמע העל.
– און עס דאַכט, אַז זי לאַכט –
פֿון דער גאַנצענער וועלט.

נאָר אַז ס׳איז טאָג געוואָרן, טאָג אַרום־אַרום –
ביים ברעג אַ מענטש האָט מען געפֿונען: טויט.
פֿון האַלדז אַ פֿלעשל האָט אַפֿאַרגעוווּנקען שטום.
נאָר פֿון זײַן אויפֿגעפֿראָפֿטן קליינעם מויל
געצויגן ווערטער האָט מען (ווי קליינע שוואַרצע שלענגלעך):
וועגן נויט,
דעפּאַרטאַצציע און וועגן גרויל. –
און. . . „דאָס זענען די סיבות פֿון מײַן טויט".
און אַ בקשה נאָך צו לעצט: פֿון „קבֿר־ישׂראל". . .

די בוכטע האָט זיך אָנגעטרונקען מיט דער נאַכט
און אַ מענטש האָט – מיט דער בוכטע.
און ביידן אויסגעמייקעט האָט פֿאַר טאָג די בוכטע.

George Raft

The man of all races, the Spanish-Mexican toreador –
his dance a vehemence, a rage within,
his vehemence a dance…
he smiles during his violent friction
and in his tenderest dance – he bites his teeth…

And like snakes struggling, his feet entwine in their steps;
he circles as he dances, stalking even as he stands still;
he flings his white partner, carries her, musses her up like a dress,
till she wrestles away from him, only to be caught up and carried
       away again;

carried away anew in their acrobatic intertwining,
limbs in tune with the rhythm, the music of blood and bone;
and during the blare of trumpets, he mutely bites his teeth,
and in a silent temper, feet, like snakes, entwine…
the man of all races, the Spanish-Mexican toreador.

Georg Raft

דער מאַן פֿון אַלע ראַסן, דער שפּאַניער-מעקסיקאַנער טאָרעאַדאָר,
ווען עמעצנס טאַנץ עס איז אַ קאַמף אַ ברויזנדער מיט זיך אַליין
און ווען עמעצנס קאַמף איז ווי אַ טאַנץ. . .
שמייכלט ער בעת זײַן העפֿטיקסטן געראַנגל
און אין צערטלדיקסטן טאַנץ – פֿאַרבײַסט ער מיט די צײן. . .

און ווי שלאַנגען אין געראַנגל פֿלעכטן פֿיס זײַנע די טריט,
אַזוי קרײַזט ער אינעם טאַנץ, אַזוי שפּרײַזט ער ווען ער שטייט;
זײַן ווײַסע פּאַרטנערין ער שלײדערט, טראָגט זי, קנוילט זי ווי אַ קלייד,
ביז זי ראַנגלט זיך אַרויס, נאָר ער דעריאָגט זי, רײַסט איר מיט;

רײַסט איר מיט און אויף דאָס נײַ אין אַקראָבאַטישן געפֿלעכט
שפּילן גלידער אויס דעם ריטעם, די מוזיק פֿון בלוט און בײַן;
און אין ליאַרעם פֿון טראָמפּײטן שטום פֿאַרבײַסט ער מיט די צײן
און אין שטילן טעמפּעראַמענט שלענגלען פֿיס זיך אין געפֿעכט. . .

155

Itshe Slutski at Ellis Island

Two months…two months…
Days…nights…
        nights…days…
        I sit and shiver.
Slutski dead to Slutski.

Water sloshes up to the concrete barrier,
    sloshes back.
I'm tossed
in the wakes of the *General Pershing*.
The sun comes from the Battery.
The tablets are under the spikes of her crown.
This island tooth off Jersey City.

Leivick, Glatshteyn – how do I find them?

I am suspended here,
but I float in a wide dissolution.

1938

Abraham Sutzkever
(1913 -)

Ant Nest

Ant nest, forest-underlife,
shattered by my curious poke,
your labyrinths, layer after layer,
fallen into dust – look,
my head falls and cracks open,
teeming with ants – words.

And each word – up, down and over,
from nerve to nerve, through serums
and spheres, then scurrying from crannies
with little white eggs in their mouths.

1940

אַבֿרהם סוצקעווער

(- 1913)

מוראַשקע־נעסט

מוראַשקע־נעסט, דו וואַלדס אונטערבאַוואוסטזײַן,
צעגישטערט פֿון אַ נײַגעריקן שטאָק, –
מיט לאַבירינטן דײַנע, שטאָק נאָך שטאָק
צעפֿאַלענע אין שטויב, זאָל דיר באַוואוסט זײַן:
ווי דו בין איך. מײַן שאַרבן פֿאַלט. אָט ווערט ער
צעטראָגן פֿון מוראַשקעלעך – פֿון ווערטער.

און יעדער וואָרט – אַרויף, אַראָפּ, אַריבער,
פֿון נערוו צו נערוו, דורך רויך און קויל.
און אַלע יאָגן פֿון די שטיבער
מיט ווײַסן אײיעלע אין מויל.

1940

[Tell]

(For my friend Rokhl Krinski-Melizin, who reminded me that I asked a surgeon in the Vilna Ghetto Hospital to let me be present at a brain operation.)

Tell me, what did you expect to see in that brain
cut open after the Jewish city had been torn to pieces?
"Maybe to see the eternal that outlasts death;
I even have a name for it: radiant core."

That skull – open. Its armor wasn't so thick.
Now – my fate – to see its radiant core.
The world at Creation must have been as clear to God –
light bearing light. Born and bare.

That skull – open. And I look into its abyss
after the old Jewish city had been torn to pieces.
Thin veins of script. I see the name-without-a-name.
I shade my eyes. I see that radiant core.

The hospital's turned dark. It's sinking to its knees.
The skull of the city is open. I've nowhere to run off to.
I'm drunk from my vision, dead drunk.
Now this radiant core will protect me.

[דערצייל]

פֿאַר מײַן פֿרײַנד רחל קרינסקי-מעלעזין, וואָס האָט מיר דערמאָנט,
אַז כ'האָב געבעטן אַ כירורג ער זאָל מיר דערלויבן בײַצוזײַן אין
ווילנער געטאָ-שפּיטאָל בײַ אַ מוח-אָפּעראַציע.

דערצייל, וואָס האָסטו זען געוואָלט בײַם אויפֿשנײַדן אַ שאַרבן
ווען שוין צעשניטן איז געווען די ייִדנשטאָט אויף שטיקער?
– מסתּמא זען דאָס אייביקע וואָס בלײַבט מחוצן שטאַרבן,
אַ נאָמען האָב איך עס געגעבן: פֿינקלענדיקער עיקר.

דער שאַרבן – אָפֿן. ס'איז דער פֿאַנצער זײַנער ניט קיין דיקער,
אַצינד באַשערט איז מיר צו זען זײַן פֿינקלענדיקן עיקר.
אַזוי האָט קעמטיק אויסגעזען די וועלט בײַם בראשית-ברא,
אַזוי האָט ליכט געבוירן ליכט. געבוירן און געבאָרן.

דער שאַרבן – אָפֿן. און איך קוק אַרײַן אין זײַנע תּהומען
ווען שוין צעשניטן איז די אַלטע ייִדנשטאָט אויף שטיקער:
דײַן אָדעריקע שריפֿט. איך זע דעם נאָמען-אָן-אַ-נאָמען,
פֿאַרשטעל איך מײַנע אויגן: ס'איז דער פֿינקלענדיקער עיקר.

פֿאַרלאָשן דער שפּיטאָל. עס נעמען קניִען זײַנע זײַלן.
דער שאַרבן פֿון דער שטאָט איז אָפֿן. כ'האָב ניט ווו צו אײַלן.
און שיכּור בין איך פֿון דער זעונג, ביז משוגע שיכּור:
אַצינד וועט מיך באַשירעמען דער פֿינקלענדיקער עיקר.

[Pasternak]

I remember Pasternak: the earth of his forelock
in fresh Moscow snow. A red scarf around his neck,
as if Pushkin had just walked in and taken over.
The snow was still on the ground.

His hand in mine, as if entrusting his key
of fingers to me. His face opposite mine – frightened
and strong. "Go on. I understand the words…sounds."
The snow was still on the ground.

I was reading my embers snatched from hell. *"A rege
iz gefaln vi a shtern."* "A *rege* fell like a star."
He followed me but couldn't grasp the *rege*.
The snow was still on the ground.

That *rege* was shining like a star in his pupils
of black marble – moist and polished. In that moment,
the Russian poet was wearing a yellow star.
The snow was still on the ground.

rege – moment

[פּאַסטערנאַק]

דערמאָנונג וועגן פּאַסטערנאַק: די ערד פֿון זיַין טשופּרינע –
אין פֿרישן מאָסקווער שניי. אַרום דעם האַלדז אַ רויטער שאַליק.
אַזוי ווי פּושקין וואָלט אַריַין... עס האָט אים וואָס געפֿאַנגען.
דער שניי איז ניט צעגאַנגען.

זיַין האַנט אין מיַינער, ווי ער וואָלט אַ פֿינגערדיקן שליסל
פֿאַרטרויט מיר. און זיַין פּנים, קעגן איבער: אי דערשראָקן
אי מאַכטיק: לייענט וויַיטער, איך פֿאַרשטיי די ווערטער, קלאַנגען.
דער שניי איז ניט צעגאַנגען.

איך האָב געלייענט מיַין גערעטעוועטן זשאַר פֿון גיהנום:
„אַ רגע איז געפֿאַלן ווי אַ שטערן" – אַלע ווערטער
פֿאַרשטאַנען, חוץ „אַ רגע". ניט געקענט צו איר דערלאַנגען.
דער שניי איז ניט צעגאַנגען.

אין זיַינע פֿיַינע פֿיכט-געשליפֿענע שוואַרץ-מירמלנע שוואַרצאַפּלען
האָט אָפּגעשטערנט יענע רגע. און זי האָט אַ רגע
דעם רוסישן פּאָעט מיט געלער לאָטע אויך באַהאַנגען.
דער שניי איז ניט צעגאַנגען.

The Woman of Marble in Père Lachaise

The woman
of marble in Père Lachaise
snared me.
It was like this:
I went to Père Lachaise
with a fresh sprig of lilac
for the remains of Chopin
turned into sounds.

The very name of the place
where the master was born –
written into the stone –
made me shudder.
When you consider the place,
he was almost a brother.
And the time?
What's a century
compared with our minutes?
God knows, I don't covet our meager present.
I put my ear to the stone
and heard: a piano raining there.

Only then, my amazed ear
felt a warm quiver,
a stirring.
I raise my head –
a woman-monument bends down to me.

די פֿרוי פֿון מירמל אויפֿן פּער־לאַשעז

די פֿרוי
פֿון מירמל אויפֿן פּער־לאַשעז
האָט מיך געפֿאַנגען.
עס איז געווען אַזוי:
איך בין געגאַנגען
אויף פּער־לאַשעז,
מיט פֿרישן בינטל בעז,
אים צו דערלאַנגען
שאָפֿענס געביין
פֿאַרוואַנדלטן אין קלאַנגען.

שוין דאָס אַליין,
וואָס אויפֿן שטיין
איז אָנגעשריבן ווי דער
מײַסטער איז געבוירן —
האָט געטאָן מיך אַ צערודער.
ווערדליק אָרט איז ער כּמעט אַ ברודער.
און ווערדליק צײַט? —
נאָר וואָס איז אַ יאָרהונדערט
אין פֿאַרגלײַך מיט אונדזערע מינוטן?
אָסור, אויב איך בין מײַן פּיצל איצטיקייט מקנא!
איך האָב מײַן אויער צוגעלייגט צום שטיין
און דערהערט: עס רעגנט דאָרט אַ פּיאַנע.

נאָר דעמאָלט האָט מײַן גאָפֿנדיקער אויער
דערשפֿירט אַ וואַרעם צאָפֿלען,
אַ באַוועגן.
אַ הייב דעם קאָפּ —
אַ פֿרוי־מצבֿה בײַנט זיך מיר אַנטקעגן.

The woman-monument come to life,
awake,
opens her lips of green mold.
She sticks her hand into my forelock
and pelts my face with her stone-speech:
"The heart I guard
left long ago for its homeland.
Only his dust blooms
in this red, dead loam.

But if you really want, monsieur,
to expend your life, like my master Chopin –
have you the slightest idea
where your heart should be taken?"

The sun shrank in my sprig of lilac,
went out.
I turned numb in Père Lachaise,
speechless:
Was it worth it to count up
some thirty years,
losing those dear to me,
hanging by a hair,
emerging from the ovens
with unburnt tears
only to hear just now at Père Lachaise
that my strong heart isn't even worth a sou?
And if I were to make a will
so someone should bring my heart home –
the entire Diaspora,
     the sad Diaspora –
               will laugh.

Paris, 1947

די פֿרוי-מצבֿה אויפֿגעלעבט און וואַך,
צעעפֿנט ליפֿן אָנגעשימלט-גרינע.
זי שטעקט אַרײַן איר האַנט אין מײַן טשופּרינע
און שטיינערט מיר אין פּנים אויף איר שפּראַך:

„דאָס האַרץ פֿון דעם וואָס איך היט
איז לאַנג אַוועק אין זײַן היימלאַנד.
און בלויז דער שטויב זײַנער בליט
אין רויטן, טויטן ליימלאַנד.

נאָר דו אַז דו ווילסט, מעסיע,
ווי מײַן האַר שאַפֿן פֿאַרברענגען, –
צי ווייסטו ווו נײַן, ווו יע,
מע זאָל דאָס האַרץ דײַנס ברענגען?"

די זון האָט אין מײַן צווייגל בעז
פֿאַרשרומפּן זיך, פֿאַרלאָשן.
געבליבן בין איך אויפֿן פֿער-לאַשעז
געליימט. אָן לשון:
כּדאַי געווען צו זאַמלען אויף מײַן קאָנטע
דרײַסיק יאָר,
פֿאַרלירן אַלע נאָנטע,
בלײַבן העֶנגען אויף אַ האָר,
אַרויסגיין פֿונעם קאַלכאויוון
מיט ניט-פֿאַרברענטע טרערן,
אַז איך זאָל איצט, אויף פֿער-לאַשעז דערהערן,
אַז מײַן אַלמאַכטיק האַרץ איז ווערט אַ פּים.
און אויב איך וועל מיר אַ צוואה מאַכן
מע זאָל שפּעטער ברענגען עס אַהיים –
וועט נאָר דאָס טרויעריקע וועלטפֿאָלק – לאַכן.

פּאַריז 1947

[Gather me]

Gather me from the ledge of time;
nest in me, like letters from a burning *siddur*.
Gather me together – I will become myself,
alone with you – our bodies entwined.

Find me in a grave, between this world and the next,
wondering which world is better....
Find me set on revenge for a single tear,
cooling my hot knife in the snow.

Think, that cloud darkens with my remains;
it bursts, with my face flashing down below.
Gather me together – I will become myself,
alone with you – our bodies entwined.

[פֿאַרזאַמל מיך]

פֿאַרזאַמל מיך פֿון אַלע העקן צײַט, פֿון שטאָק און שטײן,
פֿאַרטוליע מיך, ווי אותיות פֿון אַ ברענענדיקן סידור.
פֿאַרזאַמל־מיך־צוזאַמען – איך זאָל קענען זײַן אַליין,
אַליין מיט דיר, און דו – אין מײַנע גלידער.

געפֿין מיך אין אַ קבֿר צווישן יענער וועלט און דער,
בײַם איבערוועגן, וואָסער וועלט איז בעסער. . .
געפֿין מיך בײַם נקמה־נעמען פֿאַר אַ האַלבער טרער,
און ווען דו זעסט מיך אָפּקילן אין שניי אַ הייסן מעסער.

געדענק, אַז אויך דער וואָלקן איז פֿאַרזייט מיט מײַן געבײן,
און רעגנט מיט מײַן אויפֿגעבליצטן פּנים צו דער נידער.
פֿאַרזאַמל־מיך־צוזאַמען – איך זאָל קענען זײַן אַליין,
אַליין מיט דיר, און דו – אין מײַנע גלידער.

ABRAHAM SUTZKEVER

[Who will last?]

Who will last, what will last? A wind will last.
The blind will die, their blindness last.
The ocean's raveled foam will last.
A cloud snagged by a tree will last.

Who will last, what will last? A syllable will last,
as Creation seeds again and lasts.
For its own sake, a fiddle rose will last.
Seven blades of grass that know the rose will last.

Longer than all the northern stars will last,
the star that falls in a tear will last.
In the jug, a drop of wine will last.
Who will last, what will last? God will last.

Isn't that enough for you?

[ווער וועט בלײַבן?]

ווער וועט בלײַבן, וואָס וועט בלײַבן? בלײַבן וועט אַ ווינט,
בלײַבן וועט די בלינדקייט פֿונעם בלינדן וואָס פֿאַרשווינדט.
בלײַבן וועט אַ סימן פֿונעם ים: אַ שנירל שוים,
בלײַבן וועט אַ וואָלקנדל פֿאַרטשעפּעט אויף אַ בוים.

ווער וועט בלײַבן, וואָס וועט בלײַבן? בלײַבן וועט אַ טראַף,
בראשיתדיק אַרויסצוגראָזן ווידער זײַן באַשאַף.
בלײַבן וועט אַ פֿידלרויז לכבֿוד זיך אַליין,
זיבן גראָזן פֿון די גראָזן וועלן זי פֿאַרשטיין.

מער פֿון אַלע שטערן אַזש פֿון צפֿון ביז אַהער,
בלײַבן וועט דער שטערן וואָס ער פֿאַלט אין סאַמע טרער.
שטענדיק וועט אַ טראָפּן וויַן אויך בלײַבן אין זײַן קרוג.
ווער וועט בלײַבן, גאָט וועט בלײַבן, איז דיר ניט גענוג?

171

To the Thin Vein on My Head

I fully entrust myself to the thin vein on my head.
My word is nourished in the crystalline song of the dust.
And all the seven wisdoms the whirlwind sows
fall, without wings, like hail on a windowpane.

I love the unadulterated taste of a word, that won't betray itself,
not some sweet-and-sour hybrid with a strange taste.
Whether I rise on the rungs of my ribs, or fall –
that word is mine. A tongue burns in the black pupil of my eye.

No matter how great my generation might be – greater yet is its
        smallness.
Still eternal is the word in all of its ugliness and splendor.
To the thin vein on my head, I entrust ultimate beauty:
A wind. A clump of grass. The last star in the night.

1945

צום דינעם אָדערל אין קאָפּ

צום דינעם אָדערל אין קאָפּ פֿאַרטרוי איך זיך אין גאַנצן.
מײַן וואָרט ווערט זיך נערט אין זײַן קרישטאָליק־זינגענדיקן שטויב.
און אַלע זיבן חכמות, וואָס דער ווירבל וויל פֿאַרפֿלאַנצן –
זיי פֿאַלן אָפּ אַנטפֿליגלטע ווי האָגל אָן אַ שויב.

איך ליב דאָס וואָרט פֿון אײַן געשמאַק, וואָס זאָל אין זיך ניט פֿאַלשן,
און ניט קיין זיס־און־זויערן היבריד מיט פֿרעמדן טעם.
אַלץ איינס, צי שטײַג איך הויך אויף מײַנע ריפּן צי איך פֿאַל שוין –
דאָס וואָרט איז מײַנס. אין שוואַרצאַפּל פֿון טויט – אַ שטיקל פֿלאַם.

ווי גרויס עס זאָל ניט זײַן מײַן דור – איז גרעסער נאָך זײַן
קלייניקייט.
נאָר אייביק איז דאָס וואָרט מיט גאָר זײַן מיאוסקייט און פּראַכט.
צום דינעם אָדערל אין קאָפּ פֿאַרטרוי איך לעצטע שײַנקייט:
אַ ווינט. אַ בינטל גראָז. דעם לעצטן שטערן פֿון דער נאַכט.

1945

Deer by the Red Sea

The sunset, stubborn and brazen,
remains in the Red Sea at night,
when pink deer, innocent, gentle, come
to the palace of water to quench their thirst.

They leave their silk shadows on the shore,
and their long fiddle-faces lick
rings of coolness in the Red Sea,
and there they become engaged to silence.

Finished, they run away. Rose-flecks
animate the sand. But the sunset-deer,
mournful, remain in the water, and lick
the silence of those no longer there.

1949

הירשן ביים ים-סוף

דער זונפֿאַרגאַנג האָט זיך פֿאַרעקשנט מיט העזה
צו בלייבן אין ים-סוף ביי נאַכט, ווען עס קומען
צום פּאַלאַץ פֿון וואַסער – די אומשולדיק ראָזע,
די איידעלע הירשן צו שטילן דעם גומען.

זיי לאָזן די זייִדענע שאָטנס ביים באָרטן
און לעקן אין ים-סוף די רינגען פֿון קילקייט
מיט פֿידלענע פּנימער לאַנגע. און דאָרטן
געשעט די פֿאַרקנסונג ביי זיי מיט דער שטילקייט.

געענדיקט – אַנטלויפֿן זיי. רויזיקע פֿלעקן
באַלעבן דעם זאַמד. נאָר עס בלייבן פֿול יאָמער
די זונפֿאַרגאַנג-הירשן אין וואַסער און לעקן
די שטילקייט פֿון יענע, וואָס זענען ניטאָ מער.

1949

[So how come?]

"So how come you don't mention your Siberian father in your
    diary poems?"
A question just popped in. Instead of an answer, I only see:
before my very eyes his skin has covered my own,
and before my very eyes his beard has grown on me.

And now that standoffish son – has become his own father.
With his fingers I roll loose tobacco in a paper case.
The night is on a sparkling grindstone, ruddy and clear.
How come I know by heart page after page of the Talmud?

How come I can play the violin? I play with his fingers;
unearthly, the strings have memories of the Garden of Eden.
Whose spade is that, glazed with sparkling ice?
With his bony fingers I play on his violin.

We've become eternal in the same small space,
the old snow freshly falling and blanketing us both,
rifles and cannons no longer able to separate us.
"So how come you don't mention your Siberian father in your
    diary-poems?"

[אַלמאַי?]

„אַלמאַי דערמאָנסטו ניט אין טאָגבוך דײַן סיבירער טאַטן?"
געקומען איז אַ שאלה. און אַנשטאָט אַן ענטפֿער, זע נאָר:
פֿאַר מײַנע אויגן האָט זײַן הויט אויף מײַנער זיך באַצויגן
און אויסגעוואַקסן איז אויף מיר זײַן באַרד פֿאַר מײַנע אויגן.

אַצינד איז גאָר זײַן זון דער אָפּגעזונדערטער – זײַן טאַטע,
איך דרײ מיט זײַנע פֿינגער וויכן טאַביק אין אַ גילזע,
די נאַכט איז אויף אַ שליפֿפֿראַד אַ צעפֿונקטע, ראָזלעך קלאָרע.
פֿון וואַנען קען איך אויסנוווייניק בלאָט נאָך בלאַט גמרא?

פֿון וואַנען קען איך שפּילן פֿידל? כ׳שפּיל מיט זײַנע פֿינגער,
יענוועלטיקע די סטרונעס מיט זכרון פֿון גן־עדן.
פֿאַרשאָטן מיט אַ פֿינקלענדיקן אײַז, האָט וועמעס ריידל?
מיט זײַנע בײַנערדיקע פֿינגער שפּיל איך אויף זײַן פֿידל.

מיר זעַנען צונעאײַביקט צו די זעלבע דלת אמות,
דער אַלטער שניי האָט שניי יונגן כּוח צו פֿאַרשנייען,
צעשיידן קאָנען אונדז ניט מער קיין ביקסן און האַרמאַטן.
                                                    *
„אַלמאַי דערמאָנסטו ניט אין טאָגבוך דײַן סיבירער טאַטן?"

The Window of My Father's Store

Seasons my father couldn't afford a window dresser
he crawled in to do the job himself, his pudgy
fingers delicately tilting shoes on their stands
or positing them, pair by pair, on crystals
of fake snow or cuttings of fake grass, sometimes
roosting a sole or a heel on the vamp of its mate.
Moving on all fours and nudging along his scissors,
cardboard cylinders of ribbons, and staple gun,
he inched forward to the front pane and then inched
backwards toward the little door without upsetting
that staging of oxfords, pumps and wedgies. A vitrine,
looking like a teetotum fixed
on its point, divided the vestibule entrance in two.
I watched my father creeping behind the glass, fingering
a shoe here, flattening a run of ribbon there, or
clawing up loose staples and driving new ones in,
as if he were on display, exposed and captured there
for any passerby to see, and I wondered who is this man
on his hands and knees before me. What did his back,
neck and belly – steered by his rump – have to do with me?
On my side of those panes of glass, sealed together,
and clamped with noses of lead, I watched my father –
separate, mysterious – clipping price tags on the shoes,
dragging himself among his wares, backing toward the little door –
this man, my father – someone I neither knew nor wanted to be.

And now – tired of being bound by memory – I wonder –
what did you think when you peered out and saw me?

Poem Without a Name

I drift to a gray region, and I'm pulled
downward to the dream-entrance. Under
my sleep I awake in the Bronx Zoo. The exits
clang shut, the slams of lock-up time
in prison movies. Walkways are deserted, kiosks
shuttered, the keeper gone with his keys.

A hand with stars on its fingers moves among
the branches and writes a large R and a large F
above the cages. All their doors fling open
and the animals rush out. They pass the low
barriers and move around me. I am the one
who is trapped now, who is gaped at.

With a hairy soul and a chest smooth and black
as a bed of coal, a gorilla hulks up and asks,
"Why are you trembling so? I'm also two-footed,
and I have a heart like yours. Look, we're not
so different. I only want to feed on your death.
I only want to feast on what we have in common."

A field marshal wearing a monocle while his fingers
are tapping on a map, his swagger stick behind
his back – that's what the leopard looks like
as he strokes me with his paws. He reminds me,
"We once met at a waterhole in Zimbabwe, when you
were on safari. Now I've come to taste your poetry."

ליד אָן אַ נאָמען

אַ חלום לאָזט מיך ניט אַנטרינען פֿון זײַן לאַנגן לויער
און ווערט פֿאַרוואַנדלט אין אַ חיות-גאָרטן, ווו דער טײַער
פֿאַרהאַקט. פֿאַרשלאָסן. יאָ, אַוועק דער שומר און פֿאַרשלאָסן.
אַזאַ מין חצות איז הימל ווײַט פֿון אַלע מײַנע חצותן:

אַ האַנט מיט שטערן אויף די פֿינגער ווײַזט זיך צווישן צווײַגן
און שרײַבט אַ גרויסן אלף און אַ סמך איבער שטײַגן.
צעעפֿענען זיך שלעסער, און די חיות – נעענטער, נעענטער
צום איינציקן פֿאַרשלאָסענעם, צו מיר אַליין, דעם צענטער.

צו מיר, דעם ערד-געבונדענעם, וואָס פֿרײַ איז בלויז מײַן תּפֿילה,
דערינענטערט זיך מיט מיט האַריקער נשמה אַ גאָרילע:
– וואָס ציטערסטו? צווייפֿיסיק איז מײַן האַרץ ווי דײַנס, פֿאַרגלײַך עס –
צעקניען ווײַל איך בלויז דײַן טריט און ווײַסן אונדזער שײַכות.

אַ פֿעלדמאַרשאַל מיט אַ מאָנאָקל, טאָפֿנדיק אַ מאָפֿע –
אַזוי זעט אויס דער טיגער ווען עס צערטלט מיך זײַן לאַפֿע:
– מיר האָבן זיך באַגעגנט בײַ אַ וואַסער אין ראָדעזיע,
אַצינד בין איך געקומען צו פֿאַרזוכן דײַן פֿאָעזיע.

און ווי אַ יונגע פֿרוי מיט עולם-הזהדיקע בליקלעך,
באַגלייטנדיק איר אַלטנס אָרון, אויסגעפּוצט און גליקלעך –
אַ קאָברעשלאַנג אין שוואַרצן קלייד. זי צישעט מיר אין אויער:
– מיר זעענן בײַדע סם, און צווײַ מאָל סם פֿאַרסמט דעם טרויער.

Like a young woman, showy, thriving, with wanton glances
while accompanying the coffin of her old husband –
a cobra covered in black. She hisses in my ear:
"We're both poison, and two doses of poison poison grief."

The hand with the stars on its fingers grows dim,
this poem a remnant of the zoo-dream.
Pray. If you can still pray.
The tiger and the snake and the gorilla caged again.

די האַנט מיט שטערן אויף די פֿינגער שוויימט אַוועק אַלץ בלייכער,
פֿון חלום וועגן חיות־גאָרטן איז דאָס ליד אַ זכר:
– בן־אָדם, טו אַ תּפֿילה וואָס דו קענסט נאָך טאָן אַ תּפֿילה.
— —
צוריק אין שטייג דער טיגער און די שלאַנג און די גאָרילע.

תּל־אָבֿיבֿ, 16טן פֿעברואַר 1967

Ruvn-Yankev Fayn

(1929 -)

Miscarriage

Embryo-blood stream, membrane-outpour,
red-brown clot – you rush out of me,
my thighs soaked. I must wrap you up,
take you to the obstetrician
for tests, diagnosis, advice.
You – alive – but not among the living.
You – dead – but not among the dead.
I – a mourner – but not among the mourners –
without a gravestone, without kaddish.

To open myself up again? To receive again
the loaded heads with the whiplash tails?
Again bear the brunt of a new beginning?
Again, so conception can breed its ruin?

Better not to carry around life anymore.
To seal myself, be screwed down tight.
You, uterine-bale, tell me what to do.
You know me from the inside, you no more.

ראובן־יעקב פֿײן

(1929 -)

מפּלונג

עמבריאָן־בלוטשטראָם, מעמבראַנען־אויסגאָס,
רויט־ברוינע מאַסע – פֿלייצסטו אַרויס,
מײַנע דיקן פֿאַרנעצט. איך דאַרף דיך
אײַנוויקלען און טראָגן צום אָבסטעטריקער
אויף אונטערזוך, דיאַגנאָז און עצה.
דו, אַ לעבן נישט צווישן די לעבעדיקע,
אַ מת נישט צווישן די מתים,
איך אַן אָבֿל נישט צווישן די אַבֿלים,
אָן מצבֿה, אָן קדיש.

נאָך אַ מאָל זיך עפֿענען? נאָך אַ מאָל אַרײַננעמען
געלאָדענע קעפֿעלעך מיט שמײַסנדיקע ווײדלען?
נאָך אַ מאָל די וואָג פֿון אַ ניַעם לעבן?
נאָך אַ מאָל אַן עמבריאָן זאָל שטאַרבן?

בעסער מײַן טראָכט פֿאַרמאַכן, פֿאַרשטאָפֿן,
בעסער קיין מאָל נישט פֿאַרנײַען אין טראָגן.
דו, הײַבמוטער־קלומפּ, גיב מיר אַן עצה.
דו, וואָס קענסט מיך פֿון אינעווייניק.
דו, וואָס ביסט שוין מער נישטאָ.

185

Blue Irises

The length and width
of our bathtub –
the allotted space behind our apartment house,
time for blue folds
you planted,
you water,
you will bring into our living room.
(What do I have
to match those blossoms and colors?)
Mama, mama –
not dishes, soap, or dishtowels,
not my body or my clothes,
only blue irises
touch you now,
just as your hand touches
that bathing suit in the sepia pigment,
your bathing suit
like a gymnast's shirt and shorts.

ראובֿן-יעקבֿ פֿײַן

בלויע איריסן

די לענג און ברייט
פֿון אונדזער וואַנע
איז די גרייס
פֿונעם פּלאַץ הינטערן
דירות-הויז אויסגעטיילט
פֿאַר דיר צו האָדעווען
בלויע צוונגען און פֿאַלבן
וואָס דו האָסט באַזוימענט
וואָס דו האָסט אָנגעוואַסערט,
וואָס דו וועסט אַרײַנברענגען
אין אונדזער וווינצימער.
(וואָס האָב איך אַנטקעגן
די קוויטן און פֿאַרבן?)
מאַמע,
נישט טעלערס, נישט זייף, אָדער סטירקעס,
נישט מײַן גוף אָדער קליידער,
בלויז בלויע איריסן
קענען איצט דיך אָנרירן,
ווי דײַן האַנט רירט אָן
דײַן באָדקאַסטיום אין געל-גרויע שאָטנס,
דײַן באָדקאַסטיום וואָס איז ענלעך צו
אַ גימנאַסטקעס העמד און הייזקעס.

187

Once in a blue moon...

Once in a blue moon
a Yiddish poem comes
to me. I wish they'd come
more often. This time horns,
clefts, arcs and quadrate forms –
right-to-left majuscules the same
size my childhood eyes tried to take in
from windows and signs –
loomed the day before I came
clean and saw my name, colon,
the month, day, year on the screen
while Dr. Loewenstein was snaking within
my cecum and snicking polyps.

ראובן־יעקב פֿײן

אײן מאָל אין אַ יובל. .

אײן מאָל אין אַ יובל

קומט צו מיר אַ ייִדיש ליד.

הלוואַי וואָלטן זײ געקומען אָפֿטער.

דאָס מאָל הערנער, שפּאַלטן,

בוינגס און פֿירזײַטיקע פֿאָרמען –

גרױסע אותיות אין זײער שטראָם, רעכטס אױף לינקס,

די זעלבע גרײַס װי די װאָס מײַנע קינדעראױגן

האָבן זיך באַמיט צו באַנעמען

פֿון װיטרינעס און שילדן –

האָבן זיך דערזען אײַן טאָג אײדער איך האָב אױסגעלײדיקט מײַן

אײַנגעװײד

און איך האָב געזען מײַן נאָמען, מײַנע געדערעם,

דעם חודש, דעם טאָג, דאָס יאָר אױפֿן עקראַן,

בשעת ד״ר לעװונשטײן האָט געהאַלטן אין באַלײכטן

און אױסשנײַדן אָנװוּקסן בײַ מיר אין די געדערעם.

Abo Stolzenberg

(1905 - 1941)

Dream Canaan

(from "The Diary of a Straw Knight," the entry for Feb. 20, 1909)

Canaan? How do you get there?
In a dream it's easy to get there.
No fear of Turks, no boat or train,
just take the heel of a loaf and an apple,

jump over a fence, climb over a wall,
stride through a field, run through a garden.
I pull up my collar – a wind's blowing in from the Jordan –
and sit on a mound of sand by the gate.

Ishmaelites sweep through and snatch my cap.
I chase them and tumble into a cellar, the dirt
floor littered with seltzer bottles, Joseph on a pallet,
two snakes clang cymbals, a sallow beggar scrapes a fiddle.

Like in a dream, the cellar whirls – two saws saw
in the desert, on top of a heap of stones, not far from Beth-El.
Mother Rachel sits outside – she sees me, comes over to me.
Her spotless apron and the kerchief on her head sparkle.

אבא שטאָלצענבערג

(1941 - 1905)

חלום כנען

20סטער פֿעברואַר 1909

ווי אַזוי קען מען קומען אין לאַנד כנען? –
אין חלום איז לײַכט אַהין צו קומען.
נישט קיין שרעק פֿאַרן טערק, נישט קיין שיף, נישט קיין באַן –
אַ שישקע פֿון אַ ברויט און אַן עפּל גענומען,

אַריבערגעלאָפֿן דעם גאָרטן, אַריבערגעשפּאַנט אַ פֿעלד,
אַריבערגעקראָכן אַ פּלויט, אַריבערגעקלעטערט אַ מויער,
כ׳שטעל אויף דעם קאַלענער פֿון רעקל, פֿון ירדן ציט אַ קעלט,
כ׳זעץ זיך אַ ביסל אַנידער אויף אַ בערגל זאַמד בײַ אַ טויער.

ס׳פֿאָרן דורך ישמעאלים און ציִען מיר אָפּ דאָס קאַשקעטל.
איך לאָז זיך לויפֿן נאָך זיי און פֿאַל אַרײַן אין אַ קעלער.
פֿלעשער מיט סאַרף אויף דער ערד, יוסף אויף אַ הילצערן בעטל,
צוויי שלאַנגען שפּילן אויף אַ צימבל, אויפֿן פֿידל אַ בעטלער אַ
                                                              געלער.

ווי אין חלום שווינדלט דער קעלער, צוויי זעגן שטײַען און זעגן,
אין מידבר, נישט ווײַט פֿון בית-אל, איבער אַ קופּע מיט שטיינער.
אין דרויסן זיצט מוטער רחל – זי זעט מיך און גייט מיר אַקעגן,
ס׳בלענדט אויף איר קאָפּ די פֿאַטשיילע, ס׳בלאַנקט דער פֿאַרטעך
                                                              דער רײַנער.

She gives me mead to drink, cooks up some millet and honey.
She blesses me before I leave and slips me a few pennies
to buy cherries on the way. Hail stings me, my shoes sink into clay.
Who knows if I'll get out of this in one piece?

Like shadows, spies haul clusters of grapes on poles.
A roar – my heart's drilled into, my hair stands up.
A lion laughs, flicks a knotted tail, sizes me up.
I nod off, open-eyed, on a mound of sand, by a gate.

Birds circle back home, the summer's begun.
I run after them, they show me the way from up there.
In town, the lame beggar sits near a vaulting horse.
Pigeons flutter over roofs, sunlight floods the windows.

אבא שטאָלצענבערג

זי קאָכט אָפּ הירזש מיט האָניק, זי גיט מיר מעד צו טרינקען,
זי בענטשט מיך פֿאַרן אַוועקגיין און גיט מיר קאָרשן צו קויפֿן.
ס׳לאָזט זיך אַ שאַרפֿער האָגל, די שיך אין ליים אַרײַן זינקען,
ווער וווייסט צי כ׳וועל מיטן לעבן פֿון דאַנען קענען אַנטלויפֿן.

ווי שאָטנס גייען מרגלים מיט העננלעך טרויבן אויף שטאָנגען.
מײַן האַרץ בוויערט דורך אַ געבריל, די האָר שטעלן אויף זיך קאַפֿויער.
ס׳לאַכט מיר אין פּנים אַ לייב, – ער מעסט מיטן קנאָפּ צו דערלאַנגען . . .
איך דרימל מיט אָפֿענע אויגן אויף אַ בערגל זאַמד בײַ אַ טויער.

ס׳פֿליִען פֿייגל אַהיים, ס׳הייבט זיך אָן שוין דער זומער.
איך לאָז זיך לויפֿן נאָך זיי, זיי ווײַזן דעם וועג מיר פֿון אויבן.
אין שטאָט, נעבן באָקל זיצט שוין דער בעטלער דער קרומער,
ס׳פֿלאַטערן טויבן אויף דעכער, די זון האָט פֿאַרגאָסן די שויבן.

193

The Return of the Repressed

O, Yiddish poets,
I never guessed you could become a gift to me –
your poems could give birth to my own,
your deaths could transport us to talking,
your obsessions could translate me.
It still astounds me that you wrote at all,
that Yiddish – which I had so long relegated
to the kitchen, to smutty jokes of uncles,
to the rhinestones of aunts,
to a coarseness, a crudeness
I couldn't get rid of and had to push down –
that what was so low – that *Yiddish* –
could become the source of poetry.
Long ago I was lured by you and didn't know it,
caught by the cry of the peddler in our alley –
keshkloze, keshkloze;
by the bickering and gossiping of the wives
standing in the sawdust and pointing to the cuts
in the display case of Berman's Butcher Shop,
where the chopping table, dented and cracked,
was scrubbed and scrubbed for the next day,
where the golden dowels on the black-handled knives
were like doubloons smoothed to an obscure value.
And then I came to hear you beyond the folk,
came to see that what troubled the poets
I admired in English also troubled you – give or take a world,
a language, the people who could read you.
Yet, I confess, I'm still astounded that you wrote –
that Yiddish could turn into poetry,

its jabber pitched into lines I relish aloud.
(I know, I know, how naive all this sounds,
how you must smile at me for my ignorance,
for having kept Yiddish within the confines I assumed.)

It excites me to think of Ruvn Ayzland
tutoring the young Abo Stolzenberg
at a table at Schreiber's Cafe: "You'll find
your rhythms. You'll become subject to them."
"Watch how the wrong word turns into the right word" –
the two of them hunched over a table, just as
George and I work over our poems at Au Bon Pain,
where the converging of Mt. Auburn and Mass. Ave.
divides the traffic like a prow.
And so I have found by reading you –
by going down to the quickening dead –
that your letters are markings of me,
markings I still long to comprehend, inside
of me since childhood, and that I never grasped.
I must tell you – how important your poems are to me –
their letters still jostling into place to make sounds –
their sounds breeding in me –

O, Yiddish poets

BIOGRAPHIES

B. Alkvit-Blum (1896 - 1963)

B. Alkvit was born in Chelm, Poland. (His real name was Eleazer Blum, but he adopted B. Alkvit as his nom de plume.) Blum had lost both his mother and father by the age of twelve and was raised as an orphan, receiving the traditional religious education. After his schooling he set off to Lublin and then to Vienna, where he first experienced secular life. In 1914 he immigrated to America and worked in a sweatshop as a tailor.

In 1920 Blum published his first poem, which appeared in the avant-garde journal *In Zikh*. His early poems revealed a clear bent for expressionist and modernist images, while his later work displayed the influence of American imagist poetry and his readings of Walt Whitman, and gave voice to his concerns regarding the fate of Jewish-America during the inter-War years. His poetry appeared in many of the best American Yiddish literary journals, and from 1934-38 he was one of the editors of *In Zikh*. In 1931 he published his strongest collection of verse, *Vegn Tsvey un andere* (*About Two and Others*). He also wrote short stories and literary essays and was a contributor to the daily *Tog, Morgen Zhurnal*.

Alkvit's verse may seem minor when compared with Glatshteyn's accomplishments, but his voice is an authentic reflection of the spirit of the last generation of Yiddish poets in America.

Jacob Glatstein (1896 - 1971)

Probably the greatest of the Yiddish modernists, Jacob Glatstein was a virtuoso who drew new music from the Yiddish language and its syntax. In his poetry collections of the 1920s, he offers dizzying displays of what language can do, reveling in its multiplicities. His verses are taut expressions reminiscent of tankas and haikus, and they capture moments of simultaneity in time and space and offer flashes of insight from multiple perspectives.

Jacob Glatstein was born in Lublin, Poland, and received solid religious and traditional schooling, as well as additional secular schooling. His family sent him to America in 1914 to further his education, and in 1918 he entered the New York University Law School, where he met Nokhem Borekh Minkov and later Aron Glants-Leyeles. Rejecting the well-made aesthetic efforts of *Di Yunge* poets as impressionistic, moody trifles, the trio formed the *In Zikhistn* (Introspectivists) movement, the most modernist poetic movement in Yiddish literature. Their manifesto appeared in the first edition of their journal, *In Zikh* (1920), and Glatstein also gave voice to their movement when he published his first volumes of poetry, *Yankev Glatshteyn: Fraye Versn (Free Verse)* and *Kredos,* both of which astonished with their verbal audacity.

The *In Zikhistn* poets were voices of a new era; they were influenced by imagism, vorticism, objectivism and the echoes of expressionism in post-war Germany. But what made them truly unique was their devotion to their craft, and to the use of Yiddish as a means of expression. No noisy nationalistic Jewishness appears in their poetry, and they do not assume to speak for the Jewish people; nonetheless, their commitment to rediscovering the poetic possibilities of Yiddish argued for their strong identification with the culture. For the *In Zikhistn,* their Jewishness was as natural as a French poet's Frenchness.

Glatstein's early *In Zikhistn* poems were a product of the Jazz Age: they contain the jagged realities of post-World War I sensibilities, a world in which art for art's sake was rejected and aesthetic endeavors were open to revolutionary new approaches. Glatstein embraced free verse and believed in the liberation and wonderment of city life; urbanity echoes throughout his verses. Here was a poet who made New York the center of modern Yiddish poetry, a place more advanced and more truly modernist than either Warsaw or Moscow.

In the 1930s, Glatstein, already married and a father, felt the need to make two trips back to Lublin to see the realities of Polish-Jewish life for himself. This resulted in two remarkable novels: *When Yash Went Back* and *When Yash Returned.* His art was greatly affected by the dismal realities of Jewish life in Eastern Europe and in Europe in general. His poetry turned away from its experimentations, neologisms, telescoping of nouns, and preoccupation with the self. Instead, he focused his poetic attention on conveying the increasing agony of the Jewish people. In his 1938 poem "Good Night, World" he wrote, "I am the dust of your dust, Sad Jewish life," and this poem was to mark his return to social and moral commitments, and to his proud identification as a Jew. The war years and the aftermath of the Holocaust profoundly affected him, and he developed a strong group of narrative poems that centered around the Hasidic master, Rabbi Nakhman of Bratslav. Glatstein became an ardent defender of Yiddish culture and its role in Jewish life.

Uri Zvi Greenberg (1894 - 1981)

This giant of modern Hebrew poetry debuted as a bilingual Hebrew/Yiddish poet in pre-World War I Lemberg (Lvov). By 1921 he had moved to Warsaw, the center of Yiddish cultural life in Eastern Europe, where he joined the expressionist modernists who called themselves *Di Khalyastre (The Gang)*, the name taken from a slur made by a leading traditionalist writer.

If Hebrew became Greenberg's main vehicle for poetic expression, it happened consciously in 1923 when he abandoned his avant-garde literary journal, *Albatros*. In the final volume of this, the most cutting-edge journal ever produced in Yiddish, and published in Berlin to escape the Polish censors of the earlier two volumes, Greenberg declared that Yiddish – and European Jewry – had no future in "the Kingdom of the Cross." In fury, he cursed Yiddish as a doomed *"gasn moyd,"* a street walker, who slept with everyone she met.

In despair, Greenberg fled Europe for Tel Aviv, where he sought to build Zionism in the old homeland. Though he wrote primarily in Hebrew, his Yiddish poetic voice rang like no other: it was an organ point, fiery and dramatic, with the power and mantle of the prophets. Here one could hear the Hebrew inheritance of prophecy, a voice that was bitter, pessimistic, and lyrical beyond measure. Greenberg produced jagged, ruthless verse of titanic power, commanding the full resources of Yiddish prosody and Hasidic and kabbalistic imagery.

In his sonorous, rich verse, Greenberg accused the Gentiles of attempting to destroy Jewish life and culture, and heaped curses upon the perpetrators of the destruction that was taking place before his eyes. No other Yiddish poet approaches his rhetorical intensity or erudition; he is the only poet in Yiddish that espouses his Jewish identity with fierce pride and defends it in his verse like a shield of David. His major Yiddish poem, *Mephisto* (1921), provides the full fury of his poetic voice.

Greenberg's poetic vision seeks to restore the Jewish people to their rightful place in this world, as a unique and chosen people whose divine role is to be a "light unto the nations."

Moyshe-Leyb Halpern (1886 - 1932)

Moyshe Leyb Halpern is one of the most original poets in American Yiddish verse and certainly one of the key figures in the world of Yiddish poetry. He emerged suddenly, a totally new voice, with the publication of his first collection of poetry, *In Niu-York*, which was to prove hugely popular and rapidly went through three editions.

The poems in the collection capture the lonely, insecure existence of the young Jewish immigrant, who, having left his traditional *shtetlekh* for a new way of life, suddenly finds himself cast into the pitiless canyons of New York City.

Moyshe Leib Halpern arrived in America in 1908 from his hometown of Zloczow (Zlochev), a town he mocked in his famous poem as being one place at least in which he would never happily be buried. In New York he began publishing in the various anthologies of *Di Yunge* group, but he was never a full-fledged member; he was too independent. He developed a wonderfully singular persona, "Moyshe Leyb," who was not his alter ego but rather an extension of himself, a sort of Jewish *Til Eulenspiegel* or free spirit who marched to his own beat, and with whom the poet debated the meaning of life.

Seeking to vent the frustrations and disillusionments of the new immigrant, Halpern found escape in his nocturnal wanderings. He became a wonderful poet of the night, reaching out to the moon, the sea, and the shadowy trees, and fusing the landscape of the night with the cityscape of his daily life. His unexpected images and clashing insights often draw on the grotesque and nonsensical to give voice to these two opposing elements. His formal concerns took a backseat to his rhetorical inflections and the demands of shaping his poetic persona. He is always self-conscious, shrewd and scornful, a cheeky, challenging personality with a poetic soul. Ironic and sardonic, he never softens his perspicacious interrogations of the human condition. *Umru*, a kind of disquiet, dominates all his verse: his poetry holds no peace.

His collection, *Di Goldene Pave* (The Golden Peacock; 1924), is a fusing of physical and metaphysical encounters, and gives voice to his yearnings for a kind of lyrical state, a notion represented by the Golden Peacock, the Ashkenazic symbol of Jewish artistry. Two further posthumous volumes appeared in 1934, revealing his expanding poetic world view and his bold, startling personality. Moyshe Leyb Halpern's voice is Jewish-American, and the freedom of his expression and of his vision has no European Yiddish counterpart. No other Yiddish poet had his uniquely confident self-depreciation: the ability to mock oneself fiercely and then join in the laughter.

Izi Kharik (1898 - 1937)

Izi Kharik was considered one of the most influential Soviet poets, and for this he paid dearly with his life. Born in Zembin, White Russia, into a proletarian family of shoemakers, Kharik received a basic religious and secular education. He began writing poetry at a young age, and by 1920 he was publishing his work in a communist-oriented journal.

The vigor and easy comprehension of his poetry came to the attention of the Soviet cultural authorities and he was encouraged to leave Minsk and work in Moscow. During the Moscow years (1922-1926), he published the well-received long poem *Minsker blotes* (*Minsk Marshes*), depicting the changes in the *shtetl* during the revolution. With this work, Kharik advanced rapidly in the Soviet Yiddish literary hierarchy.

He returned to Minsk in 1926 and published *Af der erd* (*On the Land*), his first major collection of poetry. In this collection, Kharik, in down-to-earth lyric language, revealed the differences between the revolutionary life of the city and the traditional lifestyle in the country towns. He joined the editorial board of *Shtern* (*Star*), the intensely Jewish communist literary journal, and also joined the board of the newspaper *Oktyabr* (*October*), which fully supported Soviet aims but was unsure if they could be successfully implemented.

Kharik joined the Communist Party and rose to be a member of the Central Committee of the White Russian section; he was even made a member of the Presidium of the Soviet Union Writers' Union. However, he began to see that the new Soviet ideology might mean the destruction of the Jewish way of life, and a hint of ambivalence entered his worldview. His 1928 volume, the long narrative poem *Mit leyb un lebn* (*With Body and Soul*) questions delicately if the building of a socialist country will really be possible.

Poetry poured from his pen at a rapid pace, with volumes published almost annually. He had the pleasure of knowing that his poems were taught and recited in all White Russian Yiddish schools. His playful use of the language of White Russian Jewry and his skillful integration of folkloric elements created poems that were rich, colorful, and profound.

At the height of his fame and career, Kharik was arrested. He was killed in the Great Stalinist Purges of 1937, and posthumously rehabilitated in 1956.

Moyshe Kulbak (1896 - 1940)

Born in Smorgon, a large town near Vilna, Moyshe Kulbak had both a traditional and modern education and was fluent in Hebrew and Russian. During World War I he lived in Kovno, where he wrote Hebrew verse. In 1918 he moved to Minsk, and then traveled on to Vilna in 1920, where he published his first volume of verse in Yiddish.

Drawn by the vibrant cultural scene in post-World War I Berlin, he traveled to this most modern of European cities and studied there for three years. Years later, whilst living in the Soviet Union, he turned this Berlin experience into a mock epic in verse, *Disner Tshayld-harold* (*Disna's Childe-Harold* [a town in White Russia]; 1933), a jaunty, expressionist portrayal of a young Eastern European Jew living the wild life in decadent, capitalist Berlin. In this evocative work, young poets sit in cafés sipping cherry brandy and having heated discussions about jazz bands and Lao-Tzu, whilst protesting workers block the surrounding streets, their red banners held aloft. Kulbak offers a compelling account of a young, contemporary Jew who embraces modernity whilst still feeling pangs of nostalgia for a world that no longer exists.

In 1924 he returned to Vilna and taught Yiddish literature in the local high school and Teachers' Seminary. He also published two striking novellas in the fantastic mode, *Meshiakh ben Efrayim* (1924) and *Montog* (*Monday*; 1926), and one of his finest evocative long poems, *Vilne* (*Vilna*; 1926), a love poem to this quietly decaying city. Another long poem, *Raysn* (*White Russia*), depicts, with gentle humor and much grace, the ordinary Jewish country folk living amidst forests and marshes. He makes skilful use of Biblical and Slavic allusions to secure the authenticity of his account of this extended Ashkenazic family.

Kulbak was very active in the cultural life of Jewish Vilna, and his decision to depart for the Soviet Union in 1928 came as a shock. But he found life in Poland constricting and, with most of his family in Minsk, he had a strong motive for believing the Soviet Union's propaganda, which proclaimed that the communists were building new Yiddish cultural institutions.

In Minsk he wrote plays, the aforementioned mock-epic masterpiece, and another remarkable novel, the two-volume *Zelmenyaner (The Zelmenyaner Family*; 1935), in which he depicts two generations of an ordinary Jewish family being turned into model Soviet citizens. There is savage irony hidden in this text and one can only wonder that it escaped the notice of the Soviet censors at the time.

In September 1937, during the Stalinist purges, Kulbak and many of his fellow Minsk writers were arrested. One month later, Kulbak was executed.

H. Leivick (1888 - 1962)

For the Yiddish speakers of America, H. Leivick symbolized *the* Yiddish poet, a figure of dignity, gravity, and empathy. There was nothing Bohemian about Leivick: he was the very image of the serious artist, giving voice to the social and ethical concerns of the first generation of Jewish immigrants from Eastern Europe.

Leivick's childhood was one of poverty and emotional suffering, as he experienced the injustices imposed by the Tsarist regime and the immutable hierarchies of *shtetl* society. He joined the revolutionary *Bund* (Leftist Jewish socialists) shortly before the Russian Revolution, and in 1906 was arrested and sentenced to four years of forced labor and permanent exile to Siberia. That period by the river Lena haunts his poetry, and the suffering he endured there reinforced his sense of social justice. Like Dostoyevsky, Leivick viewed suffering as redemptive, especially if it led to higher standards of ethical behavior. He saw poetry as a way to celebrate and embrace the highest goals of human fulfillment.

Leivick was eventually smuggled out of Siberia with the assistance of Jewish revolutionaries, and he sailed to America in the summer of 1913. Upon arriving in New York he was plunged into the typical immigrant experience, working in the sweatshops and later as a wallpaper hanger to get by. The 1920s and 1930s saw his greatest productivity, as he published poetry collections and dramas on an almost annual basis. His verse plays, particularly *Der Goylem (The Golem*; 1921), established his name throughout the Yiddish world. In *Der Goylem,* Leivick highlighted the inherent fallibility of would-be Messiahs, reworking the familiar tale in which an artificial man, created for utopian purposes, turns against society and wreaks havoc. A later play, *Der Maharal fun Rotenberg* (*The Grand Rabbi of Rottenberg*), handles more successfully the conflict between suffering and sacrifice, and may be his finest effort in verse drama.

By 1936, Leivick, who published in many of the left-leaning newspapers – the best way for a Yiddish poet to reach an American audience – was disenchanted with communism and the *Bund*, and he accepted a position at *Der Tog* (*The Day*), the most intellectual Yiddish newspaper in New York, and one with a pro-Zionist bent. From this forum he published numerous poems and the occasional article.

The bitter realities of World War II affected him greatly. Like many Jews in America, he felt helpless when confronted with the impending extinction of European Jewry, and he gave voice to these feelings of guilt and horor in his 1945 volume (and poem) *In Treblinka bin ikh nit geven* (*I never was in Treblinka*).

Despite constant allusions to the "Old Country," Leivick was a Jewish poet in New York, and thus belongs to the New World. His verse turned New York City into a new Jewish realm, a place where Jewish life could flourish in both familiar and unexpected ways. He embraced the Lower East Side, and admired the vitality and spirit he encountered there. He understood, however, that his beloved tongue, Yiddish, the new instrument of Jewish secularism, had been destroyed in Europe and was dying in America: the purveyors of the American Dream could accept Judaism as a religious creed, but could not embrace Leivick's secular *Yiddishkayt*, a vision of a language, culture and code of ethics that was facing demise.

At its best, Leivick's poetry gathers the Jewish masses of his generation inside the warmth of *Yiddishkayt*, a language and culture suspended in an aesthetic twilight of ethical transcendence.

Mani Leyb (1883 - 1953)

Mani Leyb brought to Yiddish poetry a quiet elegance, refined diction, and a poetic voice that displayed real warmth and intimacy. He was the first Yiddish poet to appreciate and illustrate the formal qualities of poetry in Yiddish; his use of enjambment, for example, is subtle, conscious and effective. His rhymes ring clearly and add to the meaning and magic of his verse. Mani Leyb was also the first Yiddish poet to fully exploit the traditional German ballad form, fusing the lyric with the narrative in a seamless unity. Some of his ballads addressed mature topics, such as adultery and the loss of love, while others were written as chirpy, light tales for young children, offering delicious plays on words. The latter ballads were recited and sung universally in Yiddish schools all over the world. He also wrote the first significant sonnets in Yiddish, showing a full appreciation of the form and making use of astute emotional allusions.

Mani Leyb (born Mani Leyb Brahinsky) was born in the Ukraine in 1883. He came to American in 1905 and published his verse in the *Forward* and other periodicals. By the end of World War I, Leyb, Zishe Landau and Ruven Iceland were co-editing the anthologies of their poetic movement *Di Yunge* (The Young Ones). Their poetic credo eschewed the pre-War poetry of social engagement and the notion of the poet as a voice of the people. Instead, under the influences of German neo-Romanticism, late French Parnassian formalism, and Russian impressionism, they sought to create a Yiddish version of "art for art's sake," a way forward in which poetry became an intimate expression of the self, making use of formal structures and providing a strong vicarious experience through the thoughtful rendering of subtle emotions.

Mani Leyb's collected poems, *Lider un Baladn,* were published posthumously in two volumes in 1955, and his collected sonnets appeared in 1961. While he was certainly admired in his lifetime, Mani Leyb's renown as a poet has increased in the years since his death, as his formal refinements, musicality, and the enormous power of his language have become more fully appreciated. Leyb's aesthetic heir both in form and musicality – if not in profundity – is Itsik Manger, with whom Leyb also shares a certain lightness of touch.

Itzik Manger (1901 - 1969)

A self-proclaimed folk bard, Itzik Manger adopted the ballad style of German poetry to create colorful scenes of Jewish life. He achieved his fame as a poet by adopting the persona of the contemporary secular visionary, making use of the grotesque and unexpected to capture the mood of his people.

Manger arrived in Warsaw in 1928, bringing with him from Czernowitz and Jassy the earthiness of the Romanian provinces. Unlike the philosophical, highly intellectual Warsaw *Khalyastre* writers of the early 1920s (for example, Melekh Ravitch, Uri Zvi Grinberg, and Perets Markish),

Manger preferred to employ the down-home, folkloric ways of Romanian Yiddish folk bards, aligning a lightness of touch with the theatrical spirit of Goldfadn, the father of Yiddish theater.

Manger composed many volumes of verse, which were later collected into *Lid un balade* (*Song and Ballad*; 1952). He also wrote plays, essays and a colorful quasi-autobiographical novel, *The Book of the Garden of Eden* (1939). Between 1928-1938, his most productive years, he moved more deeply into the Jewish cultural inheritance and produced his masterpieces, *Kumesh lider* (*Bible Songs*; 1935) and *Megile Lider* (*Songs of the Scroll of Esther*; 1936). These volumes grew in scope, emerging in 1951 as *Medresh Itsik* (*Itsik's Retellings of the Bible*).

In the ballads of *Medresh Itsik*, Manger re-imagines the stories of the first five books of the Bible, artfully selecting heightened dramatic moments and recounting them in a lyrical voice that even Heine would envy for its ironic tone and delicacy of feeling. The poet and his family appear in the texts as cobblers (as they were in reality) and interact fully with the Biblical figures, joining them in taverns to drink and bicker. Manger mocks the norms of Jewish religious life and is unafraid to radically rework traditional portrayals of Biblical characters, offering strident critiques of characters such as Abraham and Sarah, and giving voice to often overlooked characters like Ishmael and Hagar. Manger sets the stories not only in Israel, but in the Carpathian Mountains and the plains of Southern Galicia, in the little Jewish market towns of his childhood, known in Yiddish as *shtetlekh*. And he advanced the time-setting to the years just before World War I, the era known as *Franz Josef's Zeit*, the golden twilight of Austro-Hungary, when its borders reached to the Ukraine and the Jews in this Empire – as opposed to those in the Tsarist one – enjoyed a poor but peaceful life.

This retelling of the Bible stories was nothing less than a new Jewish epic in verse, expressing the collective Eastern European (Ashkenazic) Jewish voice that Manger makes one and continuous with the past. The poems in this work share a remarkable unity of narrative voice, and the overall effect is of a modernist collusion between the poet and the reader, a celebration of Jewish tenacity, and a witty connivance of Jewish diasporic consciousness.

Manger survived the Holocaust by escaping to England and then to America, where he lived in anonymity. Only when he immigrated to Israel in 1958 did he find some psychological respite and a glimmer of the fame he once knew – but the tongue he loved, Yiddish, was already dying out. Once, in his Brooklyn stairwell, as he was carried up to his bed in a drunken stupor, he muttered, "Ikh bin a dikhter fun teyte" ("I am a poet of the dead").

Anna Margolin (1887 - 1952)

Tough, strong, and intensely personal, the poetry of Anna Margolin provides a wonderful insight into the world of the newly emergent Yiddish-speaking female poets, who, like the new generation of males, were breaking with religion and turning to socialist and nationalist visions.

A restless soul, Margolin arrived in New York from Russia in 1906 and was soon off again. She married in Palestine and had a son, but soon abandoned both husband and son forever and returned to New York in 1913. She married again and worked as an editor for *Der Tog* newspaper under the pseudonym of Anna Margolin (she was born Rosa Lebenboym).

Margolin began publishing her poems with *Di Yunge* group and later with the *In Zikhistn* (Introspectivists), and in 1929 she published her only volume of poetry, *Lider*. Suffering from crippling depression, she had stopped publishing and writing by 1932. Her common-law third husband Ruven Iceland, a leading poet of *Di Yunge* group, took care of her from then on and, in accordance with her wishes, destroyed all her unpublished verse and correspondence upon her death.

Margolin was an anarchist for much of her life, but her politics do not appear directly in her verse. For her, poetry was closer to the *Di Yunge* aesthetic that focuses on the individual author and his or her personal inner life. She sought to reveal the intensity of her desires and her attitudes to the men she met and loved. No Jewish woman before her had so openly expressed her sensual and emotional relationships to men, nor caught herself, in self-reflexive mode, ruminating on her place in the world. Her taut verse pushes aside any sentimentality or appearance of seductive femininity, revealing instead a strong will and a rich emotional understanding of the self. Her poetry shows a keen appreciation of what form and rhyme can offer the poet, and is more structured than the work of other feminist poets like Celia Dropkin and Kadie Molodowsky.

Margolin was ahead of her time in the Yiddish world, and brought a post-modernist sensibility to the feminine condition. Only in recent times have her poems been rediscovered and recognized as the authentic expressions of a modern Jewish woman.

Perets Markish (1895 - 1952)

Peretz Markish was born in Polonnoye, Volhynia (formerly part of the Russian Empire; now part of the Ukraine). As a child he attended a cheder and sung in the choir of the local synagogue. Following World War I, during which he served as a private in the Russian Imperial Army, Markish moved to Kiev and began publishing his poetry. His first volumes, *Shveln* (*Thresholds*) and *Stam* (*Simply*), caught the eye of Yeheskiel Dobrushin, a key critic, who lauded him, as did the new readers. His verse appeared lyrical, revolutionary, stentorian and fresh. However, Dovid Bergelson, the master of Yiddish prose style, considered him noisy and preferred his contemporaries, Dovid Hofshteyn and Leyb Kvitko, who would all be part of Markish's sodality: together, the trio would comprise the finest Yiddish poets in the Soviet Union, until, under Stalin's orders, Dovid Hofshteyn and Leyb Kvitko were shot on August 12, 1952.

In 1921 Markish moved to Warsaw, and he remained outside of his beloved Soviet Union until 1926, living mainly in Poland but traveling as well to Paris and even to Palestine. In Warsaw he joined with Uri Zvi Greenberg and Melekh Ravitsh to create the first modernist movement in Yiddish literature, dubbed by its enemies *Di Khalyastre* (*The Rowdy Bunch* or *The Gang*). The group embraced the name, and in 1922 they adopted it as the title of their influential new literary review.

Their poetry reflected the high point of expressionism, and Markish led the way with a brilliant declamatory style that gripped young Jewish audiences; one contemporary declared that Markish's poetry left a circle of sweat at his feet. Adored for his good looks, his passionate espousal of Soviet Bolshevism, and the drama of his expressionist verse, he became a celebrity. His new works appeared in grand editions which he later admitted were underwritten by the Soviet Embassy for his role as a paid *agent provocateur*.

In 1922 he published his masterpiece of the period, *Di Kupe* (*The Mound*), a modernist dirge that denounced the Civil War pogroms of 1919, blasphemed God, and lamented the desecrated human life piled up in the *shtetl* square. This work contrasted sharply with the idyllic nature poetry that appeared in the earlier *Volin* (1919). A prolific writer, Markish also produced children's poems; essays on the revolution and the future of Yiddish literature; and a number of longer poems evoking *shtetl* life. Returning from his trip to France, he helped set up in Warsaw the most important weekly literary revue in Yiddish, *Literarishe Bleter* (1924-1939).

His verse celebrated the beauty of nature, a new theme for Eastern European Jews. He also wrote of the wonderment of change, the need for revolution, and the necessity of saying farewell to the past. Markish was influenced by the Russian poetry of the Silver Age and the Futurists, and his prosody showed endless experimentation. He introduced syntactical innovations based on Slavic syntax, delaying the adjectives (including demonstrative and possessive adjectives) until after the nouns; stretching the verse lines; and creating new rhythms by using Russian meters such as the three unstressed short syllables and then one stressed syllable. Slavic vocabulary abounds in his verse and he uses these lexical features to stress the Yiddish cultural ties to the Slavic world and its proletarian victories. He used slant rhymes considerably and mastered free verse. At the same time, there was a classicizing effort that emerged as he sought to use traditional forms like the Romantic stanza and lyric sonnets with long verse lines.

After his return to the Soviet Union in 1926, he was pressured to conform to the demands of Soviet literature, which meant writing on approved themes such as "the noble worker." In 1929 he published a novel, *Dor Oys Dor Eyn (From One Generation to the Next)*, which was criticized for its emphasis on Jewish national identity.

Given the Order of Lenin in 1939, and made head of the Yiddish section of the Soviet Writers' Union, Markish officially joined the Communist party in 1942. His last important poem was *Tsu a yidishe tantserin (To a Jewish Dancer*, 1940), which managed the seemingly impossible task of fusing Soviet universalism with a strong sense of Jewish national identity. His final long poem, the epic *Milkhome (War)*, was less successful, with its creaky structure and strict adherence to the Party line.

In 1949 Markish was arrested for anti-Soviet activities and was shot with other poets in Lubianka prison Moscow. He was rehabilitated posthumously in 1955.

Itshe Slutski (1912 - 1944)

Born to a religious family in a *shtetl* of Eastern Poland, Itshe Slutski received the traditional religious education, but yearned for secular studies and fell in love with music. He served in the Polish Army from 1933-34, and subsequently moved to Danzig. In 1938, sensing no future in Poland, he immigrated to America, where his father was now living in Brooklyn.

Detained at Ellis Island for obscure reasons, he was sent back to Poland in 1939.

In Warsaw he published at his own expense a volume of poetry, *In mitn* (*In the Midst Of*), of which only two copies survive, both in the United States: the rest of the small run was destroyed by the Germans. Jacob Glatstein was familiar with the verse and admired its rich lines. Slutski's poetry reflects the *Angst* of the Jewish people as they confront the dark days to come. His verse is also a celebration of his love of music, and this is reflected in the evocative poems dedicated to various composers. He captures the mood of the young, sensitive poet who is yearning for fulfillment but surrounded by obstacles.

In his *shtetl* he took part in the underground defense and helped many flee into the woods, as he himself did when he joined the Soviet partisans. He fought in the marshes and forests and was killed in a skirmish in the marshes of White Russia in 1944.

Abo Stolzenberg (1905 - 1941)

Abo Stolzenberg was born in Galina, Galicia. He arrived in New York in 1923, and, like Moyshe Leyb Halpern and many other Yiddish poets, took on various jobs to keep body and soul together. He was friendly with Zishe Landau of *Di Yunge,* but also had ties to Moyshe Nadir and Halpern. He published but one volume, *Lider* (*Poems*; 1941), which contained a fine collection of poems, many in ballad form.

His poetry is vivid, with rich imagery and unexpected turns of phrase and subject. He explores the painful distance between the dream of the city and the reality of exile, and portrays the poet as a man haunted by solitude, the flight of time, and the inevitability of death. His verse is modernist in imagery and rhythm, and he has a sharp eye for the telling detail. A certain good-natured naiveté runs through his work, and his sensibility led him to subjects that were both contemporary and personal.

Stolzenberg developed testicular cancer at a young age and preferred to die rather than lose his virility. He left behind two young children and a grieving wife.

Abraham Sutzkever (1913 -)

The last living major poet of Yiddish, Abraham Sutzkever wears this mantle well: he is determined to carry on the torch of the language and its poetic culture, but is prepared to accept that it must now continue to illuminate without its progenitors.

Sutzkever was born in the small city of Smorgon, Poland. When the town was burnt to the ground by the Germans during World War I, the family fled to Omsk, Siberia, where Sutzkever's father died in 1920. His mother took him back to Vilna in 1922. The years in exile provided the poet with a certain exotic experience, which was later reflected in his volume *Sibir* (*Siberia*; 1953). In Vilna he received both a secular and traditional Jewish education, and wrote poetry in Hebrew before he began composing in Yiddish. In 1931 he became friendly with Leyzer Volf , and by 1933 he had joined with other Modernist writers and artists to form *Yung Vilne* (*Young Vilna*).

His first volume of poetry, *Lider*, appeared in 1937. It established his name and was appreciated in the *In Zikh* circles of New York. During the period in which Lithuania was dominated by the Soviets, Sutzkever published a second volume of verse, married, and had a child, who would be murdered by the Germans. When the German offensive began against Russia and they overran Vilna, Sutzkever and his wife were incarcerated in the ghetto. He participated in the ghetto resistance movement and was one of the few to escape in 1943, joining a Jewish Soviet partisan group. His poems became known in Moscow's Jewish circles and he was airlifted to Moscow in 1944, where Ilya Ehrenburg described him as "a hero of a Greek tragedy." In 1946 he published a volume of the poetry he had written in the Vilna ghetto, and he served as a witness of the Shoah in Vilna at the Nuremburg Trials. He returned to Poland with his wife and newborn child, and then traveled on to Paris, finally emigrating to Tel Aviv in 1947.

In Israel he established the quarterly *Di goldene keyt* (*The Golden Chain*), which became an influential organ of Yiddish poetry. The years in Israel brought a second bloom to this poet, and he inspired others who survived the Holocaust to use Yiddish as their authentic poetic tongue, despite the efforts of Hebraicists to deny Yiddish any validity in the new state. In his poetry Sutzkever celebrated the landscape of his new home, just as he had done in Siberia and Lithuania. He accepted his role as both a poet of witness and of personal vicissitudes, and became a national poet of Israel, a writer who gave meaning to the large historical forces at play in his own life and the lives of the Jewish people.

Sutzkever adopted surrealist imagery in his verse, and used wide-ranging registers of language and tonality. He knew old Yiddish, having translated part of the *Bovo Bukh* (a late medieval text), and he read contemporary Polish poetry too, allowing him to employ a variety of literary perspectives and poetic techniques in his work. His verse lines demonstrate his virtuosity with the language; his ear is always sure and his tone immediately recognizable. His prosody has been lauded by critics and contemporary poets alike over the last fifty years.

In attempting to address the tragedy of the Shoah, Sutzkever never yields to messianic solutions or endless pessimism, but rather offers a weary acceptance of the human condition in the universe: *ver vet blaybn, vos vet blaybn? blaybn vet a vint,...Got vet blaybn, iz dir nit genug? (Who will last, what will last? A wind will last...God will last. Isn't that enough for you?)* He is the poet *par excellence* of judicious accommodation.

Aaron Zeitlin (1899 - 1974)

Aaron Zeitlin was a dramatist, essayist, journalist and poet in both Yiddish and Hebrew. Born into an illustrious family, Aaron Zeitlin's father, Hillel Zeitlin, was a leading religious thinker during the inter-War years. He had no truck with modernism and was shocked by his son's blaspheming friends, calling them a Wild Bunch or Gang, *Di Khaliastre* – the name the friends subsequently adopted for their poetic movement. Despite their artistic differences, Aron and his father remained close, and the prosperous, colorful Zeitlin family was the envy and pride of Warsaw's Jewish community.

In the 1930s Aaron Zeitlin published a key journal, *Globus*, in which his friend Isaac Bashevis Singer debuted his prose masterpiece, *Sotan in Goray (Satan in Goray)*. This journal gathered the neo-Orthodox young writers who wanted to fuse modernist techniques with a deep commitment to the inherited values of traditional Judaism. They scorned the *Bundist* and leftist socialist fiction and sought to interpret in verse and prose profound Jewish concerns regarding man and his place in the universe.

In his poetry, the richly controlled language and mastery of expression permitted endless allusions and meanings, and Zeitlin was able to weave together his philosophical concerns and Jewish religious insights. He was heavily drawn to kabbalistic interests and allusions, and in his verse and plays the reader is granted access to a fantastical world, an unfamiliar space between the poles of myth and utopian ideals, and between settings of stripped bare purity and liturgical sumptuousness.

Shortly after traveling to America in the summer of 1939 to help mount one of his plays, Zeitlin learned to his grief that his family had been wiped out by the German invasion. He remained in America for the rest of his life. The horrors of World War II left Zeitlin with a desperate need to reconcile the destruction of Jewry with the eternal place of Jews in the schema of God. This question, and notions of time – both in its role in creation and its presence in the act of living – come to dominate his later poetry. His verse is very Judaic, and although he does not wholly embrace nationalistic Zionism, he comes close to the intellectual and religious resources that resonate in Uri Zvi Greenberg's expressionistic verse.

NOTES

"Tkhine on Operating a Stall in the Marketplace"

Tkhines (plural of **tkhine**) were very popular non-canonical Yiddish prayers in prose for women in Eastern Europe. Unlike the Psalms, they were about subjects that were part of women's everyday life. My poem is an imitation of the genre, part invention and part re-creation of material I found in a collection of **tkhines** a friend of mine inherited from his mother.

Anna Margolin

"My Tribe Speaks"

The Gemorah is the commentary on the Mishnah (the Oral Law). Together, the Mishnah and the Gemorah constitute the Talmud.

"She with the Cold, Marble Breasts"

Most of the poem is inscribed on Margolin's tombstone.

H. Leivick

"To America"

Hirsh Lekert, a shoemaker of socialist allegiances, attempted, in 1902, to assassinate the governor of Vilna, who ordered Jewish and Polish workers to be flogged for participating in a May Day demonstration.

"A Memory (I)"

According to Theodor H. Gaster, in *Festivals of the Jewish Year*, ancient Jewish law indicated that some sins could be expiated by flagellation and, therefore, pious Jews of Eastern Europe used to go to the synagogue the day before Yom Kippur and receive a token form of the punishment from a specially appointed official. The ritual, according to Gaster, "was not so much a crude, punitive act as a gesture of voluntary humiliation – an essential element of penitence and atonement."
Hayyim Schauss describes "the symbolic ceremony" in some detail in *Guide to Jewish Holy Days* (New York: Schocken Books, 1962, p. 152), noting that the flogger would lightly stroke the pious elders (men) who came to the synagogue for the ceremony.

"Father Legend"

Kislev: The Jewish month (usually overlapping with December), when Chanukah is celebrated and candles are lit.

Perets Markish

"Sadness grows in hands"

The 1923 dating marks the poem as having been written a few years after the slaughtering of Jews in the Ukraine.

BIBLIOGRAPHY

Sources of the Yiddish texts

Mani Leyb, "A Plum," from *Lider un baladn*, I, New York, 1955.

Moyshe-Leyb Halpern, "Zlotshev, My Home," "Considering the Bleakness," from *Di goldene pave*, Cleveland, 1924. "Evening," "In the World," from *Moyshe-Leyb Halpern*, New York, 1934. "You, My Restlessness," from *In New York*, New York, 1954.

Anna Margolin, all poems from *Lider*, New York, 1929, except "She with the Cold, Marble Breasts" from *Lider*, edited by Abraham Novershtern, Jerusalem, 1991.

H. Leivick, "Yiddish Poets," "Here Lives the Jewish People," "Father Legend," from *Ale verk, lider*, New York, 1940. "A Memory (I)," from *In Treblinka bin ikh nit geven*, New York, 1945. "With Everything We've Got," "To America," from *A blat af an eplboym*, Buenos Aires, 1955. "A Memory (II)," "A Small Sheet of Paper," from *Lider tsum eybikn*, New York, 1959.

Uri Zvi Greenberg, "Recognition," from *Farnakhtngold*, Warsaw, 1921. "I drink marrow and blood," from *Mefisto*, Warsaw, 1922. "In broad daylight," from *Gezamlte Verk*, Jerusalem, 1979.

Perets Markish, all poems from *A shpigl af a shteyn*, ed. Khone Shmeruk, et al., Tel Aviv, 1964.

Moyshe Kulbak, "I have seen…," from *Oysgeklibene shriftn*, ed. Shmuel Rozhinski, Buenos Aires, 1976.

Jacob Glatstein, "Great World of Quiet Wonder," from *Gedenklider*, New York, 1943. "Maybe You," "A Sunday Over New York," from *Fun mayn gantser mi*, New York, 1956.

B. Alkvit-Blum, "Your Grass," from *Lider*, New York, 1964.

Izi Kharik, "August," from *A shpigl af a shteyn*, ed. Khone Shmeruk, et al., Tel Aviv, 1964.

Aaron Zeitlin, all poems from *Gezamlte lider I, II*, New York, 1947.

Itzik Manger, "Every Morning," from *Shtern in shtoyb*, New York, 1967. "Hagar's Last Night in Abraham's House," "Abraham Takes Isaac to the Sacrifice," "The Sacrifice of Itzik," from *Lid un balade*, Tel Aviv, 1976.

Itshe Slutski, all poems from *Inmitn*, Warsaw, 1939.

Abraham Sutzkever, "Ant Nest," "The Woman of Marble in Père Lachaise," "To the Thin Vein on My Head," from *Poetishe verk, I*, Tel Aviv, 1963. "Gather me," "Deer by the Red Sea," from *Poetishe verk, II,* Tel Aviv, 1963. "Poem Without a Name," from *Firkantike oysyes un mofsim*, Tel Aviv, 1968. "Tell," "Who will last?," "Pasternak," "So how come?," from *Tsviling-bruder*, Tel Aviv, 1986.

Abo Stolzenberg, "Dream Canaan," from *Lider*, New York, 1941.

A Note on the Type

The English text of this book was set in Adobe Garamond. Designed for the Adobe Corporation by Robert Slimbach, the fonts are based on types first cut by Claude Garamond (c. 1480-1561). Garamond gave to his letters a certain elegance and feeling of movement that won their creator an immediate reputation and the patronage of Francis I of France.

The Yiddish type of this book is set in Ezra SIL, a typeface fashioned after the typography of the Biblia Hebraica Stuttgartensia (BHS), a beautiful volume familiar to Biblical Hebrew scholars.